15 STEP LES

Developing a Foundation of Faith Built on Christ

信仰の歩みを確立する 15 の基礎レッスン

Textbook|テキストブックブック

発行元 セカンドレベル・ミニストリー

2011 年 12 月　初版発行

2019 年 3 月　第 5 版発行

聖書 新改訳©2003 日本聖書刊行会

Second Level Ministry

2841 Greystone Lane, Atlanta, Georgia 30341

dainidankai@secondlevel.org

www.secondlevel.org

© 2019 Second Level Ministry All rights reserved.

All Scripture quotations are taken from New International Version.

TABLE OF CONTENTS

Learner's Guide	4
Teacher's Guide	6
Step 1 New Life - What is a Christian?	8
Step 2 Assurance of Salvation	14
Step 3 Assurance of Eternal Life	22
Step 4 The Bible is the Guidebook for Your Life	30
Step 5 Basics of Prayer	38
Step 6 How We Should Pray	46
Step 7 Sin and Temptation	54
Step 8 Understanding God's Will	60
Step 9 How to Live in God's Will	66
Step 10 The Meaning of Trials	74
Step 11 Christian Fellowship	82
Step 12 The Art of Witnessing	88
Step 13 Serving God	96
Step 14 The Importance of the Church	102
Step 15 Becoming like Christ	110

目次

学ぶ方への手引き	5
導く方への手引き	7
Step 1 新しい人生-クリスチャンとは	9
Step 2 救いの確信	15
Step 3 永遠のいのちについての約束	23
Step 4 聖書は人生のガイドブック	31
Step 5 祈りとは	39
Step 6 どのように祈るのか	47
Step 7 罪と誘惑	55
Step 8 神のみこころとは	61
Step 9 神のみこころに生きるために	67
Step 10 試練の意味	75
Step 11 クリスチャンとの交わり	83
Step 12 証人となる素晴らしさ	89
Step 13 神に仕える	97
Step 14 教会の大切さ	103
Step 15 キリストの似姿に変えられる	111

Learner's Guide

- 15 Step Lessons is a series of Bible studies that help new Christians grow in the essentials of faith and knowledge of Scripture. Each lesson is designed to help establish a good foundation for Christian living. This bilingual edition has lessons written in both English and Japanese.
- In this textbook, Scripture and additional explanations are already printed, to facilitate the study. The workbook has the same contents but includes corresponding worksheets. Both books can be used together, according to your needs.
- You can work through the lessons by yourself, but we recommend that you do them with either someone who has already completed them or a knowledgeable Christian brother or sister who can lead you. That way you can ask questions and discuss the topics. Second Level Ministry offers sessions online. If you need someone to lead the 15 Step Lessons for you and want to study together, please contact us.
- You can gain a better understanding of the lessons when you use with questions to review. (Go to the website secondlevel.org where you will find a link to the Q&A from each lesson page.)
- Please answer each question and submit the answers online. You will receive further explanation and correspondence from the Aka pen sensei*, so that you can understand each topic better.
- Please feel free to contact us if you would like to order more copies or have any questions. dainidankai@secondlevel.org

*"Aka pen sensei" literally means 'red pen teacher' and is a familiar term to Japanese people. It is used to describe someone who corresponds with participants, by providing answers and deeper explanations about the topic at hand. Counseling is also available.

学ぶ方への手引き

- 「15 のステップレッスン」は、新しくクリスチャンになられた方に役立つ基礎的な内容を中心とした 聖書の学びです。クリスチャンとして成長していくために、よい出発をするために作られています。
- 本書、メインテキストは、聖書箇所や説明が印刷されており、簡単に読み進めていけるタイプです。別冊のワークブックは、同じ内容のものが書き込み式になったものです。テキストとワークブックを共に利用していくことも可能です。
- お一人でも学べますが、すでにステップレッスンを終えられた方や、クリスチャンとして導いて下さる兄弟姉妹と一緒に学ぶと、疑問に答えてもらったり、ディスカッションをしながら進めていけます。→ セカンドレベル・ミニストリーの働きの一つとして、学びを共に進める方を推薦しています。導いて下さる方が必要な場合、ご連絡下さい。
- 復習として、「Q＆A」を解くと（セカンドレベルのウェブサイト secondlevel.org を参照）考えたり答えたりする事によって理解が深まります。それぞれのレッスンのページに行って、「Q＆A」をクリックして下さい。
- 回答し、送信ボタンをクリックしてください。セカンドレベルの赤ペン先生からの返信を受け取り、さらに学びへの理解を深めることができます。
- この冊子の追加注文やご質問等ございましたら、いつでもお問い合わせ下さい。
dainidankai@secondlevel.org

Teacher's Guide

- 15 Step Lessons is a series of Bible studies that help new Christians grow in the essentials of faith and knowledge of Scripture. Each lesson is designed to help establish a good foundation for Christian living. This bilingual edition has lessons written in both English and Japanese.
- In this textbook, Scripture and additional explanations are already printed, to facilitate the study. The workbook (with green grapes on the cover) has questions for the user to consider and space to write responses, but the Scripture and explanations are not printed to encourage for more active study and interaction with the Bible itself. Both versions of the book can be used together, according to ones needs. For example, the learner can complete the workbook before meeting with you. Then when you meet, you could use the textbook and discuss their answers from the workbook.
- The contents are an intentionally simple summary. Please supplement according to your partner's needs.
- New Christians usually have a lot of questions and are in need of spiritual support to deal with their issues biblically. In order to grow as a disciple of Christ as God desires, it is imperative to be supported in the early stages. Establishing a faith in Christ occurs by actually walking with Christ. It is not merely achieved by believing in Christ. Please teach your disciple to live in the salvation of the Lord and support their walk with Christ. Hopefully, in addition to gaining valuable knowledge, their relationship with the Lord would also deepen. Please remember that the ultimate goal is not just to finish all the step lessons, but for learners to become disciples of Christ.
- Please encourage the disciple to use the Q&A after they finish each lesson. They can understand the topic better by answering and thinking about the questions. (Please see the website: secondlevel.org) There is a link to the Q&A from each lesson page.
- Please encourage the disciple to submit their answers online. They can correspond with the aka pen sensei* and deepen their understanding about each lesson. They will receive answers for the questions and further explanations about each topic.
- Please feel free to contact us if you would like to order more copies or have any questions. dainidankai@secondlevel.org

*"Aka pen sensei" literally means 'red pen teacher' and is a familiar term to Japanese people. It is used to describe someone who corresponds with participants, by providing answers and deeper explanations about the topic at hand. Counseling is also available.

導く方への手引き

- 「15のステップレッスン」は、新しくクリスチャンになられた方の弟子訓練の基礎を目的とした聖書の学びです。基礎的な学びをされた事のない長年のクリスチャンのためにも用いて頂けます。開拓伝道や、海外にて日本人へ学びを提供する宣教師のためにも、二ヶ国語で作られています。
- 本書、メインテキストは、聖書箇所や説明が印刷されており、簡単に読み進めていけるものです。別冊のワークブックは、同じ内容が書き込み式になったものです。メインテキストとワークブックを共に利用していくことも可能です。例えば、学ぶ方は、書き込み式になったワークブックをお一人で学び、導く方と会う時には、メインテキストを用いて、御言葉や本書にて説明されている部分、また書き込まれた内容について話し合いながら、学びを進めていくこともできます。
- 内容は、意図的にシンプルにまとめられています。相手の必要と理解力に合わせて、補足を入れて下さい。
- 新しくクリスチャンになった方々は、多くの疑問があったり、聖書的にそれぞれの課題を乗り越えていくための サポートが必要です。神様が望まれているキリストの弟子として成長していくために、早い段階からサポートしていくことは非常に大切です。それぞれが持っている質問やニーズに答えていくためには、彼らを一歩一歩導いてあげることが不可欠です。キリストにある信仰の確立は、キリストとの歩みを持続する事によってです。イエス様を信じたことによってゴールを獲得したのではなく、クリスチャンとしての歩みを支え、キリストの救いの中で生きていく事を教えてあげて下さい。知識をつめこむのではなく、生きた神様との関係が深まるように、導いてあげて下さい。学びを完了する事自体が目標なのではなく、導く相手が、キリストの弟子として変えられ成長していくことを目標として下さい。
- 復習として、それぞれのレッスンが終るごとに「Q&A」をご利用下さるように励ましてあげて下さい。質問に答えたり考えたりすることによって理解が深まります。（セカンドレベルのウェブサイト secondlevel.org を参照）各レッスンのページに行き、「Q＆A」をクリックして下さい。
- 回答し、そして送信するように励ましてあげて下さい。セカンドレベルの赤ペン先生からの返信を受け取り、さらに学びへの理解を深めることができます。
- この冊子の追加注文やご質問等ございましたら、いつでもお問い合わせ下さい。
dainidankai@secondlevel.org

Step 1 New Life - What is a Christian?

 **II Corinthians 5:18**

"Therefore, if anyone is in Christ, he is a new creation; the old has gone, the new has come!"

You, who have accepted Jesus' love and grace, are a new creation! Your new life will be filled with true joy and hope (even in hardships) unlike anything else you have had! There is a wonderful change that is waiting to occur in your heart, lifestyle, and future. We pray that through your time learning His Word, you will experience His wonderful love and grace.

You became a child of God when you opened your heart and welcomed Jesus into you with faith. It is expressed as "We became Christians.", "We were made new.", or "We are saved." Please understand that 'your faith' is also given by the Lord. It is the Holy Spirit who guided you to salvation; it is God who opened your eyes and gave you faith. (Ephesians 2:8)

 **John 1:12**

"Yet to all who did receive him, to those who believed in his name, he gave the right to become children of God,"

By studying what sons of God (Christians) are, you can see how you have changed spiritually and learn how your new identity has formed. Understanding them will have a great influence upon your relationship with God, as well as all of your values.

1: Christians (children of God) are:
   a) RIGHTEOUS (We are made RIGHT with God). However, this does not mean that we become perfect or sinless, but because we have accepted Jesus, our sins are forgiven and we are treated as if we were sinless. We are completely forgiven of our sins and become righteous, which enables us to have a relationship with God. (Romans 3:20-24, Colossians 1:14, II Corinthians 5:21)
   b) HOLY. Those who receive salvation are called on to be holy. (I Corinthians 1:2)
   c) LOVED and ACCEPTED by God. (I John 4:16, Ephesians 2:13,14)
   d) GIVEN THE SPIRIT, and God LIVES IN us. (I John 4:13, I Corinthians 6:19)

Step 1 新しい人生-クリスチャンとは

📖 第二コリント 5:17
> 「だれでもキリストのうちにあるなら、その人は新しく造られた者です。古いものは過ぎ去って、見よ、すべてが新しくなりました。」

イエス様の愛と赦し（ゆるし）を受け入れたあなたは、すべてが新しくされました！これからの人生は今までの一時的な満足や幸せとは違う、本当の意味での希望と喜びで溢れています！あなたの心に、生活に、また将来に大きな素晴らしい変化が訪れようとしています。これからの学びを用いて、あなたが、神様の愛と恵みを経験できますように。

あなたが心を開き、信仰によってイエス様を心に迎えたとき、あなたは神様の子どもになりました。「新しくされる」「クリスチャンになる」「救われる」と表現しますが、そのあなたの信仰さえも神様から与えられたものであることを忘れないで下さい。神様はすべてをご存知です。あなたが救われるように導かれたのは神様です。福音に目が開かれ、信仰が与えられたことも聖霊の働きによるのです。（エペソ 2:8）

 ヨハネ 1:12
> 「この方を受け入れた人々、すなわち、その名を信じた人々には、神の子どもとされる特権をお与えになった。」

神様の子ども－クリスチャン－であることの意味について学ぶ事によって、あなたの霊的な面においてどのような変化が起こったのか、また、あなたの新しいアイデンティティーについて知ることができます。それらへの正しい理解は神様とあなたの関係の中で、そして価値観すべてにおいて大きな影響をもたらします。

1: 神様の子どもとは。。。
   a) 義（正しいもの）とされている。もちろん完璧になったり、罪を犯さない人間になったわけでは ありませんが、イエス様を信じる信仰によって、正しい者と認めて下さるのです。イエス様の赦しを受け入れているので、一切の罪から解放されています。罪がなくなってしまったという意味ではなく、罪のない者のようにみなされるのです。罪からの完全な赦しが与えられ、義とされたので、神との関係を持てるようになりました。（ローマ 3:20－24、コロサイ 1:14、第二コリント 5:21）
   b) 聖なる者とされている。救いを受け入れている者は、キリストによって特別に聖別されています。（第一コリント 1:2、第一コリント 6:11）
   c) 神様によって愛され、受け入れられている。（第一ヨハネ 4:16、エペソ 2:13）
   d) 聖霊が与えられており、神様が内に住まわれる。（第一ヨハネ 4:13、第一コリント 6:19）

e) Are able to LIVE PEACEFUL LIVES under the PROTECTION and GUIDANCE of the Lord. (Psalms 91:10-12, 38:23-24, Romans 8:28, I John 5:18)
f) Are satisfied with His blessings. (Ephesians 1:3, Colossians 2:10)
g) Are given eternal life and are able to go to heaven. (I John 5:12, John 5:24)
h) Have become a child of God and an heir. You can approach the throne of God boldly. (Romans 8:18, Galatians 4:8, Ephesians 1:13,14)
i) Are given CHRIST-LIKE CHARACTER (II Peter 1:4)

This does not mean that Christians become gods, but through knowing the Lord, we are able to become like Him. Now that you are in Christ, the image of God can truly reflect in and through our lives. This does not happen on its own and requires the Spirit to work in you through your commitment and effort to serve the Lord.

It may be difficult to understand or be thankful for these spiritual changes. From now on, you will experience the wonderful change of walking with the Lord.

After accepting Jesus, you may notice some of these changes in your heart.

- You want to know more about God.
- You want to read the Bible.
- You will repent of all the wrong you have done and wish to do good.
- You want to cherish the fellowship you have with your brothers and sisters in Christ.
- You want to spread the Word of God.

These are changes you may experience, but the time these changes occur differs for each individual. Some may have all of these changes occur in them immediately, while others may take some time. Even if none of these changes are occurring in you yet, if you repent of your sins and believe that Jesus Christ has died on the cross, you are God's child who started having a personal relationship.

- e) 神様の御守りの中で生活でき、最高の神様の導きと共に、困難がある時にも平安のある人生を送れる。（詩篇 91:10－12、38:23—24、ローマ 8:28、第一ヨハネ 5:18 ）
- f) すべての霊的祝福で満たされている。（エペソ 1:3、コロサイ 2:10）
- g) 永遠のいのちへの約束が与えられている。（第一ヨハネ 5:12、ヨハネ 5:24）
- h) 神様の子ども、相続人となった。やがて、神様が持っているものを天において引き継ぐ。（ローマ 8:18、ガラテヤ 4:8、エペソ 1:13-14）
- i) キリストの似姿に変えられていく。（コロサイ 3:9-10）

あなたが神様になるという意味では、決してありません。神様の子どもとされたことによって、神様が本来意図しておられた姿を目指し、神様に喜ばれる生き方、あり方（Being）を追求するプロセスが始まったのです。イエス様にあって生まれ変わったあなたの内に、イエス様が生きておられます。イエス様と歩めば歩む程、生きて働かれておられるイエス様のご性質があなたの内に反映されていきます。イエス様の似姿に変えられて行くことは、自動的に起こるのではないので、聖霊の働きと共にあなた自身が神様を熱心に追い求めることが必要です。

これらの霊的な面においての変化は、今すぐにすべてを理解したり感謝するのは難しいかもしれません。これから神様と共に歩んで行く中で、神様の子どもである特権や素晴らしさをあなたも体験していくでしょう。

救われてから、すぐに感じるかもしれない変化がいくつかあります。

- 神様についてもっと知りたくなる。
- 聖書を読みたくなる。
- 今までの間違った歩みを辞め、正しいことをしたいと思う。
- 神様の家族である他のクリスチャンとの交わりを大切にしたいと願う。
- まだ救われてない人に、イエス様の愛を伝えたいとねがう。

などがあげられますが、人によってこのような心の変化が起こる「時」は違います。すぐにこれらすべての思いが与えられる場合もあれば、時間がかかる場合もあります。たとえ、一つの事項も今あなたに当てはまらないとしても、罪を悔い改め、「イエス様の十字架は私自身の罪のためであった」と信じるなら、あなたは神様の子どもとして、個人的な関係を持っているのです。

2: Faith is...

 **Hebrews 11:1-3**

> *"Now faith is confidence in what we hope for and assurance about what we do not see. This is what the ancients were commended for. By faith we understand that the universe was formed at God's command, so that what is seen was not made out of what was visible."*

Together with God's guidance, you are accepted as a child of God through faith in Christ's salvation and love. Faith is not simply an emotion. One may not feel fulfilled in his present state, but his faith is still real. According to the above verses, faith in Christ consists of three parts: The first is wisdom coming from understanding the Bible, conviction of the truth, and assurance of faith.

Your faith is deepened by trusting in the promise of salvation through Jesus and believing God's word is true. As your personal relationship with Jesus deepens, your faith will grow as well.

Summary

To know and understand what it means to be a child of God is very important. You learn to know who our God is and the plans He has for each one of us. To have a solid understanding of your identity in Christ is crucial to your growth.

There may be people who do not feel any change after becoming a Christian. However, your decision to accept Jesus Christ as your Lord and Savior is by far the most important decision in your life. It has an eternal impact, as well as the way that you live in this life. Let's be thankful and accept the truth that you are a son of God. In the next lesson, we will deepen our conviction of our salvation.

To our Father in Heaven, I thank you for giving us your salvation. I thank You also for the blessing of being your child and the many blessings You will continue to supply. Please lead me so that I can become closer to you and walk with You in Your ways. Amen.

2: 信仰とは。。。

 ヘブル 11:1, 3

「信仰は望んでいる事がらを<u>保証</u>し、目に見えないものを<u>確信</u>させるものです。信仰によって、私たちは、この世界が神のことばで造られたことを<u>悟</u>り、したがって、見えるものが目に見えるものからできたのではないことを<u>悟る</u>のです。」

神様の導きの中で、イエス様の赦しと愛を受け入れた信仰によって、あなたは神様の子どもとされました。信仰とは感情ではありません。「神様が素晴らしいお方だ」と思えなかったり、あるいは今置かれている状況に対して「満足とは感じない」(等々)からといって、信仰がないわけではありません。イエス様にある信仰とは、上の聖句によると３つの部分から成り立ちます。最初は、聖書が語る事を理解し<u>悟る</u>こと、そしてそれらの事がらを<u>保証</u>し、さらには、<u>確信</u>となる、ものです。

あなたのイエス様を信じるという決心、また、御言葉の約束を信頼して、確信ある信仰を深めていきましょう。信仰とは、イエス様との個人的な関係が深まるにつれ、成長していくものです。

まとめのことば

神様の子どもであることの意味を知っておくことは大切です。神様がどういうお方なのか、また神様があなたに持っていて下さる計画などを理解することができます。クリスチャンとしてしっかりとしたアイデンティティーを持つことは、神様とあなたの関係の中で大きな影響をもたらし、またあなたの霊的な成長とも深く関係していきます。

クリスチャンになっても、何も感じない人もいるでしょう。ですが、あなたがイエス様を受け入れた決心は、人生の中で最も大切な決断だったのです。それは、この世での歩み方、そして永遠を左右するものだからです。今、神様の子どもとされている事実を感謝して受け入れましょう。そして、次の Step 2 でも、さらに確信を深めていきましょう。

天の父なる神様、私にも救いを与えて下さってありがとうございます。今、私も神様の子どもとされて、これからたくさんの祝福を用意して下さっていることをありがとうございます。これから、あなたのことを良く知り、あなたに近づいて歩めるようにどうぞ導いて下さい。アーメン。

Step 2 Assurance of Salvation

 **Ephesians 2:8**

"For it is by grace you have been saved, though faith - and this not from yourselves, it is the gift of God -"

So many wonderful changes have occurred since you have accepted Jesus Christ. If you have truly repented and accepted God's love and forgiveness, salvation can never be taken away from you. Your salvation was attained through your faith in God and His grace and not from a temporary emotional experience. But anyone can have doubts. Have you ever wondered whether you are truly saved? Felt that God doesn't love you? Or worried that your actions have caused God to abandon you? Do not worry because such doubts are completely normal. The truth of God's word is not influenced by human thoughts and emotions.

In order to walk closer with God, it is important that you form a firm understanding about your salvation and realizing that it cannot be taken away. The Bible clearly states that God wants us to have confidence in our faith as we follow Him. God wants you to live with assurance and confidence.

1: Conviction through the Bible.

 Romans 8:38-39

"For I am convinced that neither death nor life, neither angels nor demons, neither the present nor the future, nor any powers, neither height nor depth, nor anything else in all creation, will be able to separate us from the love of God that is in Christ Jesus our Lord."

God will never leave you and His love will always be with you. Read these verses, think through them, and pray that you may be able to believe them.

Also look at Jeremiah 33:3, Proverbs 3:5-6. If you know that the Bible is the Word of the trustworthy God, then you can believe that everything written in it is the truth. Ask for God's help in being able to understand the truth.

Step 2 救いの確信

 エペソ 2:8

「あなたがたは、恵みのゆえに、信仰によって救われたのです。それは、自分自身から出たことではなく、神からの賜物です。」

イエス様を信じ、救いを頂いて、たくさんの素晴らしい変化が起こりました。救いは、一時的な感情の体験ではなく、神様の恵みとあなたの信仰によってもたらされたのです。一度、心から悔い改め、神様の愛と赦しを受け入れて新しく歩む人生の決心をしたのなら、救いはあなたから取り去られません。なぜなら、救いは「神からの賜物（無料のギフト）」であり、一方的な恵みとして神様がすでに与えてくださったものだからです。しかし、誰にでも疑いや迷いが起こる事があります。「本当に救われているのだろうか」「神様が自分を愛しているなんて感じない」「あんなことをして神様に見捨てられたにちがいない」等と思ったことはありませんか。心配しないで下さい。そのような不安は、新しくクリスチャンになった人にとって珍しいものではありません。

日本人にとって文化と習慣の中で体験してきた「神」は、聖書が語る神とは全く別のものです。「困った時の神頼み」「罰当たり」「因果応報」などの仏教や神道を起源とした典型的な考え方は、日本人の価値観に染み付いています。そのような思考を持って聖書の神様を見るなら、間違った神概念を持ったままでクリスチャン生活を送ってしまいます。ですから創造主である聖書の神様がどのようなお方なのかを学び続けることが大切です。そうすると、恵みに満ちた神様がどのように私たちを愛しておられ、神の子として扱ってくださるのかを理解できます。救いの御手で守られ、クリスチャンとして生きていく素晴らしさを体験できます。その一歩一歩の歩みによって、救いの確信は高められて行きます。

御言葉の真理は、人間の感情や考えによって左右されるものではありません。クリスチャンとして確信をもって神様に近づくために、まず自分が救われていることを確認し、そして神様が与えて下さった救いは失われない、と理解することはとても大切です。聖書ははっきりと、あなたの救いについて確信を持てること、また神様ご自身が、あなたにしっかりとした確信を持って歩んでほしいと望んでおられることについて語っています。それらについて、この章で学んでいきましょう。

1: 聖書から確信を得れる。

 ローマ 8:38-39

「私はこう確信しています。死も、いのちも、御使いも、権威ある者も、今あるものも、後に来るものも、力ある者も、高さも、深さも、そのほかのどんな被造物も、私たちの主キリスト・イエスにある神の愛から、私たちを引き離すことはできません。」

神様はあなたから離れません。神様の愛もあなたといつも共にあります。
これらの聖句を読み、反芻し、心から信頼できるように祈りましょう。その他、エレミヤ 33:3、箴言 3:5-6 も見てみましょう。聖書が信頼できる神様の御言葉であるとわかるなら、その中に書かれていることを絶対なる真理として受け止めれるのです。真実が理解できるように、神様に助けを求めましょう。

2: Understanding the differences between God as a creator and gods accepted in Japan

 **Acts 18:24-25**

"The God who made the world and everything in it is the Lord of heaven and earth and does not live in temples built by human hands. And he is not served by human hands, as if he needed anything. Rather, he himself gives everyone life and breath and everything else."

 **Acts 4:12**

"Salvation is found in no one else, for there is no other name under heaven given to mankind by which we must be saved."

God of the Bible is the only God. He is not a deity to go to pray to only when you need something. Even though the world changes, God does not change His mind or leave you alone. He keeps all of His promises and will continue to protect you with His love (Jeremiah 31:3). Rest assured that you were guided by this loving God and that true salvation was brought to you. God, who is the Creator of this world, is worthy to be trusted.

3: Through your daily repentance, discover God's strength through His presence!

 **James 4:8**

"Come near to God and he will come near to you. Wash your hands, you sinners, and purify your hearts, you double-minded."

Isaiah 41:10

"So do not fear, for I am with you; do not be dismayed, for I am your God. I will strengthen you and help you; I will uphold you with my righteous right hand."

Just because you've become a Christian and have faith, doesn't mean that you become sinless. When you humble yourself and return to God, He forgives your (all of your) sins (I John 1:9). However, there are times when you don't feel that your relationship with God has been restored, even after confessing your sins. When you feel that way, you should believe in the truth taught in the Bible rather than depend on your feelings. God is with you no matter your circumstances, and loves, leads, and blesses you. Pray without ceasing, repent of your sins, and believe that – as scripture says – God is now with you.

2: 日本人の神概念との違いを理解する

📖 **使徒の働き 18:24 – 25**

「この世界とその中にあるすべてのものをお造りになった神は、天地の主ですから、手でこしらえた宮などにはお住みになりません。また、何か不自由なことでもあるかのように、人の手によって仕えられる必要はありません。神は、すべての人に、いのちと息と万物とをお与えになった方だからです。」

📖 **使徒の働き 4:12**

「この方以外には、だれによっても救いはありません。世界中でこの御名のほかには、私たちが救われるべき名としては、どのような名も、人間に与えられていないからです。」

神様とは、唯一のお方です。聖書が語る神様は、困った時だけお願い事をしに行くような存在ではありません。世の移り変わりとともに、考えを変えるようなお方もありませんし、あなたを裏切るようなこともされません。約束されたことはすべて守られ、あなたを永遠の愛で守り続けます（エレミヤ 31:3）。この愛の神にあなたは手を差し伸べられ、救いを受け入れたことを再度確認しましょう。創造主なる神様は、私たちの信頼全てに値するお方です。

3: 日々悔い改める事によって、神様との親しい交わりに戻れる

 ヤコブ 4:8

神に近づきなさい。そうすれば、神はあなたがたに近づいてくださいます。罪ある人たち。手を洗いきよめなさい。二心の人たち。心を清くしなさい。」

 イザヤ 41:10

「恐れるな。わたしはあなたとともにいる。たじろぐな。わたしがあなたの神だから。わたしはあなたを強め、あなたを助け、わたしの義の右の手で、あなたを守る。」

クリスチャンになって信仰を持ったからといって、罪を犯さなくなるのではありません。神様は、あなたがへりくだって、神様のところへ戻る度、その罪を（またすべての罪を）赦して下さいます（第一ヨハネ 1:9）。しかし、罪の告白をしても、神様との親しい関係を取り戻せた気がしない時もたくさんあります。そのような時でも、感情に頼ってはいけません。聖書が教えている真理を信じましょう。神様はあなたがどのような状況の中にいても、あなたと共におられ、あなたを導き、愛し、祝福したいと願っておられます。絶えず祈り、罪を悔い改め、御言葉によって「神様は私と今共におられる！」と確信しましょう。

Also, as we saw in Step 1, anyone who is in Christ is recognized as a child of God (John 1:12). You should not submit yourself to God out of feelings of guilt, but remember that you are already accepted and loved by God, who is waiting for you to return to him.

4: Through sharing the Word, you know that the Spirit lives within you!

 I Corinthians 12:3

> *"Therefore I tell you that no one who is speaking by the spirit of God says, "Jesus be cursed," And no one can say, "Jesus is the Lord," except the Holy Spirit."*

God's Spirit has been working within you ever since that day you prayed to accept the Lord as Savior. Whenever you doubt your faith, try saying aloud "Jesus is Lord". Also, share the grace God has given you with other Christians.

 I John 4:13

> *"We know that we live in him and he in us, because he has given us of his Spirit."*

In order to live a life led by the Spirit...

Your life will not become automatically prosperous just because you have been saved.

You will have a new start as a child of God, but to live a life filled with God's grace, you must first get to know this God who desires the best life for you.

- Read the Bible and learn more about God (Step 4)
- Pray (Step 5 and 6)
- Be a part of a church/body of Christ (Step 14)
- Have fellowship with other Christians (Step 11)

また、Step 1 でも見たように、キリストを救い主として受け入れたあなたは、神様の子どもとされました。(ヨハネ 1:12)。罪悪感から、あるいは神様に受け入れられるために従順になろうとするのではなく、愛を持ってあなたが戻ってくるのを待って下さる父なる神様に、あなたはすでに受け入れられていることを覚えていて下さい。

4: 真理を口にすることによって、聖霊が自分の中におられることがわかる

📖 **第一コリント 12:3**
> 「。。。神の御霊によって語る者はだれも、「イエスはのろわれよ。」と言わず、また、聖霊によるのでなければ、だれも、「イエスは主です。」と言うことはできません。」

そうです、あなたがイエス様を受け入れる決心をして、信仰告白した（祈った）時も、神様があなたの内ですでに働いておられたのです。自分がクリスチャンである確信が薄れた時、声に出して「イエスは主です。」と言ってみましょう。また、神様の恵みをまだクリスチャンでない周りの人々や、他のクリスチャン達と分かち合いましょう。

📖 **第一ヨハネ 4:13**
> 「神は私たちに御霊を与えてくださいました。それによって、私たちが神のうちにおり、神も私たちのうちにおられることがわかります。」

神様の御霊に導かれる人生を送るためには、、、

救われて自動的に人生が豊かになるわけではありません。神様の子どもとしての新しいスタートをきりましたが、あなたに最善な道をご用意されている神様の真理をよく知っていくことによって、神様ご自身を体験し、また、神様の恵みに満ちた歩みをさせて頂けるのです。

- 聖書を学び、神様との歩みを体験しましょう。(Step 4 を参照)
- 祈りましょう。(Step 5, 6 を 参照)
- 教会（キリストの体）の一部となりましょう。(Step 14 を参照)
- 他のクリスチャンと交わりの時間を持ちましょう。(Step 11 を参照)

Summary

Do not rely on your emotions, the situation, your accomplishments, or other people for salvation. You are already saved by your faith in the Lord and by His grace. Have confidence in the truth written in the Bible. Pray that the Holy Spirit will guide you o the conviction of your salvation. Be joyful in your salvation. Your new life with God will be overflowing with hope.

Lord Jesus, thank You for giving me salvation that will never be taken away from me. Please help me stand on a strong foundation of faith and have confidence in my salvation. If I were to doubt you, please give me the understanding and the help I need to prevent me from losing my way.

まとめのことば

あなたの救いに関して、感情、状況、行い、また人に頼ってはいけません。あなたは、神様の恵みとあなたの信仰によって救われたのです。聖書に書かれている真実に信頼しましょう。聖霊によって、救われている確信が与えられるように祈りましょう。神様の子どもとされた喜びに満ちた人生を送りましょう。神様に導かれるあなたの人生は希望であふれています！

　　主イエス様、永遠に失うことのない救いを私にも約束して下さってありがとうございます。私が救われていることを心から確信し、固く信仰に立って歩めるようにどうぞ助けて下さい。疑いがでてきた時には、間違った道に行くことがないように、どうぞ必要な理解と助けを与えて下さい。アーメン。

Step 3 Assurance of Eternal Life

 John 10:28

> *"I give them eternal life, and they shall never perish; no one can snatch them out of my Father's hand."*

Are you ready for eternity? Unless faced with death, most people will not have thought much about eternal life or heaven. Are you that person who thinks he will never be involved in a fatal accident? Have you never dreamed that you may die from disease? Our life is very fragile and you will never know when it may end. It could even be today or tomorrow!

If you have accepted Christ and have been saved, you are promised eternal life. It means that Christ, who is the eternal life, lives within you, so you are spiritually alive. Even if your flesh dies, your soul will continue to live in a spiritual form. Because you were redeemed by Christ, your relationship with God is restored and eternal life results. (It's also imperative to understand that you need to walk with Christ and to know Him while on this earth. See John 18:3 as well.) Having confidence in God's promise will bring a great change in your life as a Christian.

In Step 2, we were clearly told through the Bible about our promise in salvation. In this lesson, we would like to develop the confidence in the truth that salvation = eternal life. Also, let's try to understand the importance of living our life in a worthy manner as a saved person. First, let's look at why confidence in our eternal life is so important.

1: Results from Assurance of Eternal Life
   a) You have joy. (I Peter 1:8, 9)
   b) You no longer fear death so you have peace. (Philippians 4:8)
   c) You have hope even after death since you know you will go to heaven. (II Thessalonians 2:16)
   d) You have purpose in what you do because you are storing up treasures in heaven - treasures that will not perish, unlike the treasures of this world. (Matthew 6:20)
   e) You have perseverance to go through the trial of this world by knowing that your citizenship is in heaven. (Philippians 3:20)
   f) You know that you will be rewarded for your trials in life with the crown of life. (James 1:12).
   g) Our identity is found in eternity belonging to the life of Christ.

All these things will help strengthen your life as a Christian. The Spirit will give you confidence, joy, peace and hope so that they may enjoy a full Christian life.

Step 3 永遠のいのちについての約束

📖 ヨハネ 10:28

「わたしは彼らに永遠のいのちを与えます。彼らは決して滅びることがなく、また、だれもわたしの手から彼らを奪い去るようなことはありません。」

あなたは永遠についての備えができているでしょうか。今、死に直面しているのでなければ、たいていの人は死後や永遠のいのちについてあまり考えないでしょう。「自分に限って交通事故などには遭わない」「自分に限って早死にするはずがない」と、どこかで思っているかもしれません。しかし、この世の命というのは本当にはかなく、いつ終わりが来るのかわかりません。今日か明日かもしれません。

イエス様を信じて本当に救われたなら、あなたには永遠のいのちが約束されています。イエス様が内住され、霊が生かされた状態にあり、永遠に神様と共にいる事ができます。肉体が死を迎えても、魂は永遠に生きます。あなたはイエス様の十字架でのゆるし故、父なる神様と正しい関係を持てるようになったので、永遠に神様の子である事が約束されています。(ですが、肉体の死後の「永遠」というだけではなく、今現在、いのちであるイエス様があなたの内に住まわれて、この人生を生きるという理解が大切です。ヨハネ 18:3 参照。) 永遠のいのちが与えられていることへの確信は、神様の子どもとしての歩みの中であなたに大きな変化をもたらします。

Step 2 では救いの確信について聖書からはっきりと教えられました。ここでは、救われている = 永遠のいのちの約束があることを明確に理解していきましょう。そして、救われている者としてふさわしい歩みをしていくことの大切さ、またその称賛としても与えられる永遠のいのちについても見ていきます。本題に入る前に、まず、なぜ永遠のいのちへの理解が大切かを見てみましょう。

1: 永遠のいのちに対する理解は、信仰生活へ大きな影響をもたらす

a) 神様と共に歩む喜びがある。(第一ペテロ 1:8-9)
b) 死に対する不安や恐怖から解放され、平安のある人生が送れる。(ピリピ 4:8)
c) 永遠に神様と一緒にいられると知ると、死後の行き先に希望がある。(第二テサロニケ 2:16)
d) 死後だけでなく、この人生においての働きも、宝を天に蓄えているという希望と目的がある。(一時的な、あるいは無意味な人生ではなく、生きる意味をもつ)(マタイ 6:20)
e) 自分の国籍が天にある(ピリピ 3:20)事は、この世での辛さや試練に耐える力となる。
f) この世での報酬を、いのちの冠(ヤコブ 1:12)として頂けると確信できる。
g) 「永遠」というキリストのいのちに属する者としてのアイデンティティーが生まれる。

これらすべては、クリスチャンとして生きる力となります。聖霊を通して確信が与えられ、喜び、平安、希望などを心から経験できるようになるでしょう。「永遠」という視点は、あなたの生き方を大きく変えていくのです。

2: Confidence in Your Eternal Life

The Bible clearly states that if you were saved through your faith, then you have eternal life. If you truly believe that the Bible is the Word of God, then you probably will not doubt that everything in it is true. Eternal life can't be felt or seen right now, so it's normal to feel that we only halfway understand it. Living with an assurance of eternal life is very important. Let's look at what the Bible says about eternal life.

a) Christ came to this world so that you may have eternal life.

 **John 3:16**

> *"For God so loved the world that he gave his one and only Son, that whoever believed in him shall not perish, but have eternal life."*

b) Whoever believes in Christ has eternal life.

 **John 5:24**

> *"Very truly I tell you, whoever hears my word and believes him who sent me has eternal life and will not be judged but has crossed over from death to life."*

Other scriptures - John 3:36, I John 5:12

c) Eternal life can never be taken away from you.

 **John 10:28**

> *"I give them eternal life, and they shall never perish no one can snatch them out of my hand."*

Other scriptures - Romans 8:33-39, John 6:39

d) The Lord wants you to have assurance of your eternal life!

 I John 5:13

> *"I write these things to you who believe in the name of the Son of God so that you may know that you have eternal life."*

2: 永遠のいのちに関して理解できる事

救いの確信について学んだことと平行している部分がたくさんあります。聖書には、信じて救われ、神様に喜ばれる生活をしている者には、永遠のいのちが確かであることが書かれています。聖書が神様の言葉であると理解できるなら、その中にある内容はすべて真実である事が理解できるでしょう。永遠のいのちは、今実感したり見たりできるものではないので、半信半疑になるのも普通かもしれません。けれども、上記 1: のセクションでもあげられているように、永遠についての理解はクリスチャン生活の中でとても大切です。御言葉が永遠のいのちについて、何と言っているのか見てみましょう。

    a) キリストがこの世に来られたのは、あなたが永遠のいのちを持つためだった。

 ヨハネ 3:16

    「神は、実に、そのひとり子をお与えになったほどに、世を愛された。それは御子を信じる者が、ひとりとして滅びることなく、永遠のいのちを持つためである。」

    b) キリストを信じる者は永遠のいのちを持っている。

ヨハネ 5:24

    「まことに、まことに、あなたがたに告げます。わたし（キリスト）のことばを聞いて、わたしを遣わした方を信じる者は、永遠のいのちを持ち、さばきに会うことがなく、死からいのちに移っているのです。」

— その他、ヨハネ 3:36、第一ヨハネ 5:12 参照

    c) 永遠のいのちは、決して奪われない。

ヨハネ 10:28

    「わたしは彼らに永遠のいのちを与えます。彼らは決して滅びることがなく、また、だれもわたしの手から彼らを奪い去るようなことはありません。」

その他、ローマ 8：33－39、ヨハネ 6：39 参照

    d) 神様は、あなたが永遠のいのちを持っていることをあなたに確信してほしい。

第一ヨハネ 5:13

    「私が神の御子の名を信じているあなたがたに対してこれらのことを書いたのは、あなたがたが永遠のいのちを持っていることを、あなたがたによくわからせるためです。」

3: Desire to Live in a Manner Worthy of Salvation

It's clear from the Bible that God has promised eternal life to those who have been saved. Therefore, we must live in an appropriate way as new creatures in Christ. In Luke 10:25-28, Jesus answered a scholar of the law by saying, "Love the Lord your God with all your heart and with all your soul and with all your strength and with all your mind, and love your neighbor as yourself." Mark 12:29 calls this the greatest commandment. If we love God, we are to live in obedience to His word.

You are to continue bearing fruit as God's child by following His will. The promise of eternal life isn't an excuse to sin by thinking you can do anything you want because you already have eternal life. Instead, it should bring an awareness of "Therefore, go and sin no more.", desiring what God wants you to do.

> *To learn more about following God's will, look at Step 8 and 9, "What is God's will?"*

 **I Timothy 6:12**

> *"Fight the good fight of the faith. Take hold of the eternal life to which you were called when you made your good confession in the presence of many witnesses."*

As people born into a new life, we are to throw away our old selves and be changed by Christ into a new way of life. Rather than simply listening to Jesus, we must live it out (James 2:22). As it says in Matthew 8:21, at the end of the world people who did not follow God's will call out "Lord, Lord," to whom Jesus will answer, "I never knew you." As God's children who have received salvation, let's live as people who follow Jesus' word.

3: 受けた救いにふさわしく生きた神様の子どもに与えられる永遠のいのち

神様が、救われた者に永遠のいのちを約束して下さっていることは聖書から明らかです。だからこそ、神様の子どもとして、それを得るにふさわしい生き方、ふさわしい姿になっていくことが大切です。「何をしたら永遠のいのちを自分のものとして受けることができるのですか」という律法学者の問いに対して、「心を尽くし、思いを尽くし、力を尽くし、知性を尽くしてあなたがたの神である主を愛せよ。またあなたがたの隣人をあなた自身のように愛せよ。」を実行しなさい、そうすればいのちを得る、とイエス様は言われました（ルカ 10:25－28）。マルコ 12:29 では、これは「一番大切な教え」だと書かれています。神様を愛するなら、神様のおっしゃることに聞き、実行していく必要があります。神様のみこころを行い、実を結び続ける神様の子どもであることが大切です。永遠のいのちの約束を「救われているから何をしてもいい」と罪を犯す口実ではなく、神があなたに望まれていることを求め、「だからこそ罪を犯してはならない」と意識するべきでしょう。

みこころを行うことについては、Step 8, 9「神のみこころとは」を参照。

第一テモテ 6:12

「信仰の戦いを勇敢に戦い、永遠のいのちを獲得しなさい。あなたはこのために召され、また、多くの証人たちの前でりっぱな告白をしました。」

新しく生まれ変わった者は、古い自分を捨て、イエス様によって変えられた新しい歩みをしていくことができます。神様が言われることを聞いて終わるのではなく、御言葉を実践するべきです。（ヤコブ 2:22）「永遠のいのちを獲得しなさい」とは、救いの完成に至りなさい、という意味です。マタイ 8 章 21 節からの内容にあるように、「主よ、主よ」と求めてはいても、みこころに従わない者達は、「あなたのことは知らない」と世の終わりに神様に言われてしまうのです。永遠のいのちを約束された神様の子どもとして、イエス様の声に聞き従いながら歩んでいきましょう。

Summary

Pray to God to help you accept what He tells us through the Bible. Even if you are not ready to accept it fully, pray that He will help you to understand these things. Then the Spirit will work through your prayers and open your spiritual eyes. Christians have an immeasurable hope and peace because they are the only ones who have the privilege of being with the Lord eternally. Know that you are promised a way to heaven and be filled with praise! In light of that, let's remain in Jesus who guides us to the eternal kingdom.

I thank you Lord for preparing the way to heaven and providing eternal life for me. I thank you for Jesus and His cross. Thank you for giving me new hope to live. I have nothing to fear in this world, so help me lead my life so that I may have hope and store my treasures in heaven. Amen.

まとめのことば

神様がおっしゃっていることを、あなたも信仰を持って受け入れれるように祈りましょう。もしまだよくわからなくても、「理解できるように助けて下さい」と祈るなら、聖霊が働き、あなたの霊的な目を開いて下さるでしょう。永遠に神様と共にいられるという約束は、大きな希望であり平安です。イエス様の十字架を信じる者には、永遠のいのちへの道が用意されている約束を知り、救われているという現実に感謝と喜びを持ちましょう。そして永遠の御国へ導いて下さるイエス様の中にとどまり続けましょう。

　　　イエス様が十字架にかかって下さったことにより、私にも救いの道を与えて下さり、永遠のいのちが与えられる約束をありがとうございます。生きる希望を与えて下さって感謝します。この世のものに恐れるのではなく、天に希望と宝を積めるような人生が送れるように助けて下さい。
アーメン。

Step 4 The Bible is the Guidebook for Your Life

 **II Timothy 3:16-18**

> *"All scripture is God-breathed and is useful for teaching, rebuking, correcting, and training in righteousness, so that the man of God may be thoroughly equipped for every good work."*

An important part of Christian growth is reading the Bible. The Bible is a fascinating and wonderful book, and by reading it you are taught truth. Your mistaken ideas are pinpointed and corrected, enabling you to walk truthfully with God. As the one and only book of God's Word and truth, it serves as a guidebook for your life, and you will certainly be blessed by receiving its wisdom.

Also, the Bible is not just an advisory book, but is an ultimate truth. Seek what God desires for you, instead of taking advantage of the verses that you like. In faithful walk with God, He has great plans for you. Experience Him and His blessings for you!

The blessings received from the Bible are related to your growth as a Christian. You grow as you know about God and God's will for your life. There are no other greater things (Philippians 3:8). He desires you to know these truths. In the relationship with Him, you will become more like Christ (spiritual growth).

 **I Peter 2:2**

> *"Like newborn babies, crave pure spiritual milk, so that by it you may grow up in your salvation."*

1: By reading the Bible...

a) You can learn about God.

The Bible teaches who God is. When you become a Christian, your image of God is probably unclear and you might hold your own ideas about Him. However, if your faith is in a god based on your image, it is just a god you created. It is impossible to know who God is and have faith in Him without learning the Scripture.

Knowing God's nature has a big influence on how you live your life. For example, God says that "you are precious and honored in my sight, and I love you" (Isaiah 43:4). God is the creator of the universe but because he loves us, we don't have to compare ourselves to others and are able to have confidence in Him. Let's experience Him daily.

Step 4 聖書は人生のガイドブック

 第二テモテ 3:16-18

> 「聖書はすべて、神の霊感によるもので、教えと戒めと矯正と義の訓練とのために有益です。それは、神の人が、すべての良い働きのためにふさわしい十分に整えられた者となるためです。」

クリスチャン（神様の子ども）の成長にとって、聖書を読むことは必要不可欠です。聖書は魅力的で不思議な本です。聖書を読むことによって、真実を教えられ、間違った事を戒められ、矯正され、正しく歩むために訓練されるのです。聖書は神様の御言葉と真実で満ちた唯一の本ですから、あなたの人生の指針を示すガイドブックになることでしょう。

また、聖書は単なるアドバイスの本ではなく、その中には絶対的な真理が秘められています。好き勝手に好きな言葉だけを人生の益のために利用するのではなく、神様が望まれていることを知り、それを熱心に追求して行く必要があります。みこころを求める信仰に基づいて、神様は祝福を必ずご用意して下さっています。是非、聖書から神様について知り、神様を体験する祝福を受け取って下さい。

聖書から受ける祝福とは、「神様の子どもとして成長していくこと」であると言えます。神様の子どもとして成長するとは、神様がどのようなお方かを知り、あなたにどのような歩みを求められているのかを知って行く道のりです。これほど素晴らしい事は他にはありません（ピリピ 3:8）。神様はあなたに祝福を与えていることを知ってほしいと願っておられます。神様との歩みを深めていく中で、キリストに似た者に変えられていく（霊的に成熟した大人になっていく）のです。

 第一ペテロ 2:2

> 「生まれたばかりの乳飲み子のように、純粋な、みことばの乳を慕い求めなさい。それによって成長し、救いを得るためです。」

1: 聖書を読む事によって、、、

    a) 神様について知る事ができる。

神様がどのようなお方か、聖書ははっきりと教えています。クリスチャンになってもまだぼんやりと「神様ってこういう方だ」と自分なりのイメージを持っているかもしれません。しかしあなたのイメージにもとづいた神様への信仰なら、それはあなたが自分で作り上げた神様でしかありません。聖書を学ばずして、聖書が語る唯一の神様について知り、信仰の歩みを続けることはできないでしょう。神様のご性質を知ることは、あなたの生活に大きな影響があります。例えば、「わたしの目には、あなたは高価で尊い。わたしはあなたを愛している。」（イザヤ 43:4）という御言葉から、「創造主である神様が私を愛しておられるので、自分自身が価値ある尊い存在である。」と思えるようになります。聖書を読み、学び、研究し、神様とはどのようなお方かを知り、日々の神様との交わりの中で神様ご自身を体験していきましょう。

b) You can learn about God's will for your life.

God's will is His plan and His desires for your life. Because God's way is one of absolute love and grace, His plans exceed our human thoughts and goals.

When it comes to learning God's will for your life, you aren't restricted to your own judgments and values but can follow the way of God's magnificent plans.

You can find a better way. Your past successes and accumulated knowledge are probably based on your own determination. You know good things for your life, but God's plans are for the best things. Knowing God's will is necessary in order to choose the way with the greatest blessings.

To learn more about following God's will, look at Step 8 "Understanding God's will" and Step 9 "How To Discern God's Will"

So continue to read the Bible, desire God and His will, and God will show you how to think and live your life. This is a process by which you grow and change which continues throughout your whole life. The Bible becomes your treasure as it continues to be your guidebook over the course of your entire life.

c) It will help you be able to resist temptation and sins God hates.

As is written in I Peter 5:8-9, the enemy will try to deceive you. To deal with temptation and sin, you must know God and live for the fulfillment of His will. You must be aware of Satan's temptation and be strengthened in the spirit through God's word (Ephesians 6:10-18).

To learn more about temptation, look at Step 7 "Sin and Temptation".

2: Deciding to read the Bible

 **Matthew 4:4**

"Man does not live on bread alone, but on every word that comes from the mouth of God."

a) Read it every day!

Devotions are when you read the Bible, pray, and set aside time for God. Just as you eat food every day, you need the spiritual food of God's word which is necessary to gain energy and grow. Try to read the Bible for just five or ten minutes every day. It's important to make it a habit.

b) 神様のみこころについて知ることができる。

みこころとは、神様が望まれていること、神様のご計画です。絶対的な愛と恵みの神様が望まれている道ですから、私達の人間的な思いや計画よりもはるかに優れているものです。

人間の性質、神様と人間の関係、神様の恵みなども含めて、あなたの人生への神様のみこころを学ぶ事ができます。自分の価値観や、限られた視野での判断ではない神様の素晴らしい計画の道を歩ませて頂けます。

あなたはよい道や歩み方を知っているかもしれません。過去の成功や、積み上げた知識や経験に基づいて、自分の決断に自信があるかもしれません。あなたの計画は「よいもの」かもしれませんが、神様のご計画とは「最高のもの」と言えるでしょう。又「絶対的なもの」でもあります。みこころを知るとは、最高の祝福を選択し、神様に喜ばれる生き方をするために必要なことです。

みこころを行うことについては、Step 8「神のみこころとは」と Step 9「みこころを知るために」を参照。

聖書を読むことを通して、神様を知り、神様のみこころを知り、あなたがするべきこと、考えるべきこと、歩むべき道が示されるのです。神様ご自身やみこころを知っていくことも、あなたの霊的成長も、あなた自身の変化も一生かけて行われていきます。聖書はあなたの一生涯を通しての絶対的なガイドブック、宝物、又なくてはならないいのちの言葉となるでしょう。

c) 誘惑や神様が嫌われる罪に立ち向かいながら生活できる。

あなたをだまそうとする敵が、生活の中にあふれています(第一ペテロ 5:8-9)。神様ご自身を知り、みこころにかなう歩みをするためにも、誘惑や罪へ立ち向かう必要があります。サタンの誘惑への意識を持ち、御言葉に立って、霊的に強められていく必要があります(エペソ 6:10-18)。

誘惑については、Step 7「罪と誘惑」を参照。

2: 聖書を読む決断

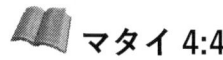 **マタイ 4:4**

「人はパンだけで生きるのではなく、神の口から出る一つ一つのことばによる。」

a) 毎日読みましょう！

聖書を読み、祈り、神様と自分のために特別に取り分ける時間を「デボーション」といいます。食事を毎日とらなければ生きられないように、霊的な面においても神様の言葉によって毎日活力を得、成長していく必要があります。1週間に一度まとめて読むのではなく、5分でも10分でも良いので、毎日読むようにしましょう。習慣づけていくことが大切です。

b) Decide on a time to read it!

Schedules vary from person to person, so pick a time for yourself when it's easy to read. There are probably many occasions when you have a little bit of time. Mornings are a good time to have devotions. At the beginning of the day you can quiet yourself before God and pray for him to guide you. Also, if you have time before going to bed you can finish your day by looking back and confessing sins and giving thanks to God.

c) Make a place you can be alone!

It's easy to be distracted in places with lots of people. If you have a roommate or are married and have children, you need to take some time to be alone. It's important to have a place where you can come quietly before God.

It's easy to mistake the Bible as being a thick, hard-to-read book. Pray for understanding as you read the Bible. Find a devotion style and way to read the Bible that suits you. Start with the Gospels in the New Testament. Below is a suggested order for reading.

b）読む時間を決めましょう！

人によってスケジュールはまちまちです。あなたにとって、読みやすい時間を決めましょう。「手があいたときに」では長続きしない場合が多いでしょう。朝は、デボーションを持つために適しています。一日のはじめに神様の前に静まり、その日、神様があなたを導いて下さるように祈ります。また、寝る前にも少し祈る時間を持つと、一日を振り返り、罪を告白し、感謝を捧げて終えることもできます。

c）一人になれる場をつくりましょう！

他の人がいる所では気が散ってしまいます。ルームメイトがいたり、結婚していたり、子供がいると余計に一人になれる場を作る努力が必要です。神様の前に静まるために、一人の場所は大切です。

聖書を読む必要性を理解し、読み続ける決断ができたでしょうか。聖書は厚くて難しい本だと思われがちです。神様が御言葉への理解を助けて下さるように、祈りつつ読んでいきましょう。あなたにあった読み方、デボーションの持ち方を見つけて下さい。新約聖書の福音書（マタイ、マルコ、ルカ、ヨハネ）から読んでいくと、比較的わかりやすいですし、下記にあげられている、読みやすい順番も参考にしてみて下さい。

Summary

Scripture is our spiritual nourishment (Matthew 4:4), it lights our paths (Psalm 119:105), and is a necessary weapon against various challenges in our lives (Ephesians 6:18). By believing and following the Bible you experience various changes in your life. Through encountering God and the Bible, your life's trajectory is changed and you can live a life in God's grace. Even if you read the Bible over your whole life, there will probably still be things you don't understand. When you can't understand, you should pray that God will help you understand and continue to read. Also, if they've made reading a habit, challenge to 'learn'. When the Word takes root in your heart and you apply it, you are being changed in a real sense.

God of wisdom and grace, thank You that You teach how I should live as I continue to read the Bible. I pray that You will grant me patience to keep reading the Bible and live a life that glorifies you. Help for me to understand these things one at a time. Amen.

Suggestion

If you're not sure where to read from the Bible:

You may want to consider reading the following order, beginning with John's Gospel.

1. The Gospel of John (New Testament)
2. The Gospel of Mark (New Testament)
3. Ecclesiastes (Old Testament)
4. 1 John (New Testament)
5. Ephesians (New Testament)
6. Acts (New Testament)
7. James (New Testament)
8. 1 Peter (New Testament)
9. Colossians (New Testament)
10. Genesis (Old Testament)

まとめのことば

聖書の言葉は霊的な食べ物（マタイ 4:4）であり、道を照らす光であり（詩篇 119:105）、また人生における様々なチャレンジで必要となる剣（エペソ 6:18）でもあります。御言葉をよりよく理解し、握り締めて歩むことによって、生活に様々な変化が出てきます。神様と出会い、また聖書と出会って、あなたの人生も軌道修正されて神様の恵みにみちた生活が始まりました。一生涯聖書を読み尽くしても、わからないことはまだまだあるでしょう。理解できない時には「理解できるように助けて下さい」と祈りながら読んでいくとよいでしょう。また、「読む」習慣がついてきたら、「学ぶ」ことも挑戦して下さい。御言葉を心に蓄え、「適用」していく時に、本当の意味であなたは変えられていくのです。

知恵に満ちておられる神様、私がどのように生きるべきか聖書を通して教えて下さり、ありがとうございます。あなたがどのようなお方か知るために、またあなたに喜ばれる人生を送るために、続けて聖書を読んでいく忍耐を与えて下さい。一つひとつのことを理解できるように助けて下さい。アーメン。

聖書をどこから読もうか迷っているあなたへ

ヨハネやマルコの福音書からはじめ、下記のような順番で読んでいくと、比較的わかりやすいでしょう。

1. ヨハネの福音書　（新約聖書）
2. マルコの福音書　（新約聖書）
3. 伝道者の書　（旧約聖書）
4. ヨハネ第一の手紙　（新約聖書）
5. エペソ人への手紙　（新約聖書）
6. 使徒の働き　（新約聖書）
7. ヤコブの手紙　（新約聖書）
8. ペテロ第一の手紙　（新約聖書）
9. コロサイ人への手紙　（新約聖書）
10. 創世記　（旧約聖書）

Step 5 Basics of Prayer

Ephesians 6:18

"And pray in the Spirit on all occasions with all kinds of prayers and requests."

1: About prayer...

Prayer is a conversation with God. It's a way to fellowship with God. It's like a breath of air for your spirit. Our mighty God is the creator of this world and all life within it.

Although He is mighty, God loves us and calls us friend. He desires to bless us abundantly. As Christians it is a privilege to pray to God. Because Jesus forgave our sins and became a bridge between God and us, we can become closer to God.

God gives us true peace, joy, and hope when we spend time with Him. Our bodies need to breathe air, and our spirits are no different. Praying to God and reading the Bible is like breathing for our souls. Having an intimate relationship with God is more important than anything else. For a Christian, the purpose of prayer is not just speaking what you wish to say or getting what you want. Prayer is fellowship and communication with God, and more importantly, continuing to learn who God is. Knowing God isn't simply an intellectual understanding, but gaining a deeper relationship with Him by realizing that He is Lord, father, and friend. As we learn more of who God is, we will understand God's will and how we ought to live (including decisions and questions) in accordance with this knowledge.

There are no regulations of how to pray. You can close your eyes, stand or sit or raise your hands in the air. You can pray while walking or driving; you can talk to God anytime. It should be our goal to live our lives in prayer, instead of finding prayer time in our lives.

Step 5 祈りとは

📖 エペソ 6:18
「すべての祈りと願いを用いて、どんなときにも御霊によって祈りなさい。」

1: 祈りとは、、、

祈りとは、「神様との会話」「神様と共にいること」又「霊の呼吸」などと言われています。

この世を創造された大いなる神様は、あなたを愛され、あなたを友と呼ばれ、あなたに最大の祝福を受けてほしいと願っておられます。祈りを通して神様との会話を持てるのは、クリスチャンの特権です！イエス様があなたの罪をゆるし、神様とあなたの罪による溝を埋めて下さったからこそ、大いなる神様にあなたは近づけるようになりました。

神様と共に過ごす時間を通して本当の「平安」「喜び」「希望」が与えられます。体にとって呼吸が不可欠なようにあなたのスピリット（霊）も、聖書を読んで糧を得、祈りを通して呼吸をし、生かされることができます。神様との親しい交わりに、他に勝るものはありません。クリスチャンにとっての祈りとは、言いたいことを一方的に話したり、お願い事を達成するのが目的ではありません。「祈る」という神様とのコミュニケーションを通して、神様と交わり、さらに神様がどのようなお方か知り、体験していきます。神様について知的に知るだけではなく、深められつつある関係の中で、主として、父として、又、友として神様ご自身を知っていきます。神様がどのようなお方か知るにつれて、みこころとは何か、またあなたがどのような歩み（選択や追及するものも含め）をするべきか悟っていくことにつながります。

祈る時に「こうしなければいけない」という規制はありません。静かに目を閉じても、座っていても立っていても、手を合わせても、歩いていても、運転していても、いつでも神様に話かけてよいのです。生活の中に祈りがあるのではなく、祈りの中に生活があるような生き方が目標です。

2: Contents of Prayer

The contents of prayer can be summarized as follows:

>A (adoration) - Praising God, adoring and worshiping Him
>C (confession) - Confessing Sin
>T (thanksgiving) – Being grateful
>S (supplication) - Requesting

Adoration: We cannot help praising Him, "For great is the Lord and most worthy of praise, He is to be feared above all gods." (Psalms 96:4) As we experience God and His works, those thoughts will be enhanced. Praise Him in your prayers. "He is the one you praise; he is your God." (Deuteronomy 10:21)

Confession: We can restore our intimate relationship by confessing our sins. "If we confess our sins, he is faithful and just and will forgive us our sins and purify us from all unrighteousness." (I John 1:9)   Knowing that we have already been forgiven, according to God's Word, we should humble ourselves before God and confess our sins.

Thanksgiving: All good things are given by Him, and nothing is ours. So why not give thanks to Him? Give thanks that God's grace isn't something that happens by chance, but is consciously given to you (including people and circumstances). In addition, you'll naturally be led to give thanks to God for the magnificence of being saved. (James 1:18, I Thessalonians 5:18)

Supplication: We can pray about our desires, plans, and struggles. "Do not be anxious about anything, but in everything, by prayer and petition, with thanksgiving, present your requests to God." (Philippians 4:6)

In addition to praying for yourselves, it is important to pray for other people. "And the prayer offered in faith will make the sick person well; the Lord will raise him up. If he has sinned, he will be forgiven." (James 5:15) Jesus said that the greatest commandment is to "love God and love your neighbor." It's impossible to have love a person without desiring the best for them. Praying for those around you is proof of that love. Jesus Himself intercedes for us (Romans 8:34). If you are able to pray for your neighbors (even our enemies), God rejoices (Matthew 5:44).

2: 祈りの内容

祈りの内容は、例えば下のようにまとめることができます。

   A (adoration) – 神様をほめたたえる、あがめる、礼拝
   C (confession) – 罪の告白
   T (thanksgiving) – 感謝
   S (supplication) – 願い事

<u>A</u>doration: 神様は偉大なお方ですから、「あなたはすばらしいお方です」とほめたたえずにはいられません（詩篇 96:4）神様について、また神様のなさることを体験するにつれて、その思いは高められていくでしょう。祈りの中で神様を賛美しましょう。
「主はあなたの賛美」（申命記 10:21）です。

<u>C</u>onfession: 罪に気づいたらすぐに告白することによって、神様との親しい交わりに戻り続けることができます。（第一ヨハネ 1:9）すでにゆるされていることを御言葉から確信しつつ、神様の前にへりくだって罪を言い表わしましょう。

罪については、Step 8「罪と誘惑」を参照。

<u>T</u>hanksgiving: 神様こそが、すべての良いものを与えて下さるお方です。偶然あなたが持っているのではなく、神様があなたへの恵みとして意図的に与えて下さったもの（機会や人なども含め）を思い、感謝を捧げましょう。さらには、救われていることの素晴らしさや、神様ご自身についての感謝を捧げる思いへも自然に導かれるでしょう。（ヤコブ 1:18、Ⅰテサロニケ 5:18）

<u>S</u>upplication: まだわからない将来や今ぶつかっている問題などに対する願い事を神様に祈りましょう。ほしいものがいつも与えられるわけではありませんが、神様はあなたの必要をご存知で、あなたにとっての最善を必ず与えて下さいます。（ピリピ 4:6）

頭文字の「ACTS」とは、「行動、業」という意味があります。

またこれらに加えて、「とりなしの祈り」（人のために祈る）といい、人のためにとりなしていくことも大切です。（ヤコブ 5:15）イエス様は、一番大切な戒めとして「神を愛し、隣人を愛しなさい。」とおっしゃいました。相手を知らずに、また相手の最善を願わずに「愛す」ということは不可能です。あなたの周りの人についての祈りは、愛の証です。そして実は、イエス様もあなたのためにとりなして下さっているのです（ローマ 8:34）。誰かのために（それが嫌な相手だとしても）祈るなら、それは神様に喜ばれることでしょう。

3: Why pray?

God knows your prayers even before you pray. God knows what is in your hearts, your circumstances, your desires, and even your future. (Matthew 6:25-34). So if God already knows everything, why is it so important to pray to Him?

Because...

- The Bible teaches us to pray. (Ephesians 6:18-19)
- God may use prayers to communicate to you and speak to your heart. (Matthew 6:6, I Peter 5:8)
- Prayer shows our trust in God. (Proverbs 3:5,6, I Peter 5:8, Philippians 4:6)
- We love God. (Psalms 116:1)
- God turns His ear to us. (Psalms 116:2)
- God receives glory by answering prayers. (John 14:13) etc...

Prayer can help you to have a better understanding of God. When you have a conversation with a friend, you learn many things about him, such as what kind of person he is or what he is thinking about. Prayer is a way for you to have fellowship with God and to experience His presence. Through prayer you communicate with God and become closer to Him. Wait for His answers while enjoying fellowship with God. Open your ears to what God has to say. When God is trying to work in your lives, it requires your obedience to what He calls you to do.

3: なぜ祈るのか

神様はあなたが祈る前からすべてのことをご存知なのです。あなたの心の中も、状況も、願いも、将来の行く道もご存知です(マタイ 6:25－34)。ではなぜ祈る必要があるのでしょう？

- 聖書が祈るように教えているから（エペソ 6:18）
- 神様とのコミュニケーションのため（マタイ 6:6、第一ペテロ 5:8）
- あなたが神様に信頼している証拠であるため（箴言 3:5-6、第一ペテロ 5:8、ピリピ 4:6）
- 神様を愛するから（詩篇 116：1）
- 神様が耳を傾けて下さるから（詩篇 116：2）
- 神様が栄光を受けるため(ヨハネ 14:13)、など。

これらすべての理由は、「神様を知るために」とまとめれるでしょう。あなたの友達とも会話をすればするほど、その人がどういう人で何を考えているかなどを少しずつ知っていきます。同様に、祈りは神様との交わりですから、その中で神様の臨在（りんざい：共にいること、存在すること）を感じ、神様が語られることを受け取り、神様ご自身についてもっとよく知れます。神様との交わりを楽しみながら、答えを待ちましょう。神様がおっしゃることに耳を傾け、確信を持って、その語りかけに応答していきましょう。人の人生に神様が介入される時、行動を起こしていくことが要求されます。

Summary

God knows your need and everything about you. However, when you pray, you are trusting in God and relying on Him. When your gracious God answers our prayers, you know it's because of Him (God Himself receives the glory.) It may be a good idea to try a Prayer Journal, with a line separating the page. You can write your prayer requests on the left, and how they were answered, how your prayers or heart were changed, etc. on the right side.

More than anything, God wants you to know Him. He wants you to receive His grace abundantly. When you don't know what you pray for, Spirit and Christ Himself intercedes for us. (Romans 8:26, 34) Pray and pour out your heart as if you are talking with your best friend! In the next lesson, you will learn how to pray in more detail.

Lord Jesus, You were nailed on the cross and took the punishment I deserve. Our Father sent You to be the bridge to enable me to have a personal relationship with Him. I thank You for it, Jesus. Thank you for always watching over me. Please guide me every day of my life. In the name of Jesus, Amen.

まとめのことば

神様はあなたの必要をすべてご存知ですが、あえて祈るのは、自分の力で物事を行うのではなく、「神様を信頼している」信仰を行動に移すことになるからです。そして、祈ったからこそ、答えが与えられた時に、「恵み深い神様のおかげだ（ご計画）」と、その答えを受け入れることができます（神様が栄光を受ける）。

「祈りのジャーナル」をつけてみるのもよいでしょう。ノートを用意し、真ん中に線を引きます。左に祈りの課題、右にはどのように答えられたか、どのような心の変化、また祈りが変えられて来たか、などを書き留めます。

神様は、あなたに神様ご自身を知ってほしいと願っておられます。また、何よりも、ご自身の恵みをあなたに受けてほしいと願っておられます。祈るために技術が必要なわけではありません。どのように祈ったらよいか分からない時も、御霊が、そしてイエス様が、私たちのためにとりなして下さっています（ローマ8：26、34）。祈りという神様とのコミュニケーションを用いて、心を神様の前に注ぎましょう！

次のStep 6で、どのように祈るのか具体的に学んでいきましょう。

主イエス様、あなたが十字架に架けられ、父なる神様と私の橋渡しをして下さったから、祈りを通して神様との個人的な関係を持つことができます。感謝します。どんな時もあなたを見上げて、祈りながら生活できるように導いて下さい。アーメン。

Step 6 How We Should Pray

1: Attitude When Praying

There is not really an exact way to pray. In the Bible, there are many prayers and many ways to pray. Let's see what the Scriptures say about it. Please refer to the Bible for the verses below.

a) Pray in the name of Jesus. (John 14:13)

"And I will do whatever you ask in my name, (ask in the name of Jesus) so that the Son may bring glory to the Father. You may ask anything in my name, and I will do it." When we pray we must pray in the name of Jesus because He removed obstacles that separate God and people. (Details in 2: Guides to Prayer, a) When praying to God you must pray in the Name of Jesus.)

b) Pray to God as your Heavenly Father. (Matthew 6:9)

In the prayer Jesus taught us, He begins "When you pray say, Father God." There is only one Living God. Our God is alive. If you pray to another god or an idol, it is idolatry. (Details in 3: The Lord's Prayer.)

c) Pray in the spirit. (John 14:16-18, Romans 8:26, Ephesians 6:18)

Even when we don't know what we should pray about or exactly in what way we should pray, the Holy Spirit will help us. So, we can rely on the Holy Spirit to speak on our behalf as we pray.

d) Pray with faith and trust. (Mark 11:24, James 1:6)

The Bible, that is the true word of God, says He will answer our prayers when we ask Him. So we should pray without doubt in our hearts and we should pray with a sense of enthusiasm. Pray for God's best whenever your prayers are unanswered and you've carefully considered if you're praying with the wrong motives. Let's seek God's best.

e) Pray with patience and eagerness. (Matthew 8:8, 8)

Sometimes it takes time for your prayers to be answered, because God's timing is best. So we should always continue to pray with patience.

f) Pray unceasingly. (Colossians 4:2, I Thessalonians 5:18)

Prayer is not about simply asking God for something that we want. It is a way for us to confess our sins, to give thanks to Him, to mediate, and to have intercession with Him. We should keep this in mind as we pray (Step 5:2 Contents of Prayer). Constant prayer brings joy to God.

Step 6 どのように祈るのか

1: 祈る態度

こう祈らなければいけないという形式はありませんが、聖書にはいくつかの模範として祈りの姿勢が述べられています。下の事項を順に見て行きましょう。聖書箇所も一緒に開いて下さい。

a) イエス・キリストの名を通して祈る（ヨハネ 14:13）

イエス様が大きな犠牲を払われた十字架によって、あなたと神様との仲介をして下さったので、あなたは神様に近づくことができるのです。神と人とを隔てていた障壁は取り除かれました。ですから「イエス様のお名前によって祈ります」と、言葉と心で確信を持って祈ることができるのです。（以下「2: 祈る際の注意点」の「a)キリストの御名によって祈らなければいけない」を参照。）

b) 父なる神に対して祈る（マタイ 6:9）

イエス様が、このように祈りなさいと示して下さった主の祈りの初めにも「天にいます私たちの父よ」との呼びかけがあります。この世を創造した偉大な神様であり、今も生きて働かれる唯一の神様です。他の何かに祈るならば、それは偶像礼拝になってしまいます。（以下「3: 祈りの模範－主の祈り－」を参照。）

c) 御霊によって祈る（ヨハネ 14:16－18、ローマ 8:26、エペソ 6:18）

何をどのように祈ってよいかわからないときも、あなたの助け主である御霊が助けてくれます。御霊の働きに、心をゆだねながら祈りましょう。

d) 信頼して、信じて祈る（マルコ 11:24、ヤコブ 1:6）

絶対の真理である聖書は、祈りに答えて下さる神様は「良きお方だ」と語っているのですから、疑わずに熱心に祈りましょう。祈っても答えられない時には、「悪い動機」で願っていないか吟味し、神の視点での「最善」を求めましょう。

e) 忍耐して、熱心に祈る（マタイ 8:8-8）

祈りが答えられるには、時間がかかることもあります。神様はすべての事柄に完璧なタイミングを持っておられますから、忍耐して祈り続けましょう。

f) 絶えず祈る（コロサイ 4:2、第一テサロニケ 5:18）

祈りは願い事だけではなく、神様への賛美、罪の告白、感謝、とりなしも含まれます。

（Step 5「2: 祈りの内容」を参照）絶えずこれらの思いと共に祈りを捧げる事は、神様に喜ばれています。

g) Pray without secrets or reservation. (Matthew 6:8)

God knows everything about you along with all your problems, anxiety, and doubts. God even knows about your future. It's not necessary to pray with ornate words. So when you pray, give yourself to God and don't hold anything back in your prayers. In being honest with God, you're able to entrust Him with your problems and accept your own weaknesses. As you open up yourself, there will be things that you discover about yourself as God speaks to your heart.

h) Pray specifically. (Philippians 4:6, I Peter 5:8)

God knows everything about you; praying specifically means that you are entrusting each thing to God. You may experience specific answers to your prayers.

i) Pray in private. (Matthew 6:6)

When you received Christ and were saved, you started a personal relationship with Him. Let's make it a priority to spend time alone with God. God is pleased when you spend time with Him.

j) Pray with a group. (Matthew 18:20)

Praying with your brothers and sisters in Christ is also wonderful thing. You will develop unity as God's family as you pour out your requests to God. Praying for one another results in love. When you receive prayer for others you'll be encouraged. Where two or three or more are gathered in His name, God will be in the midst.

2: Guides to Prayer

The Bible says that God listens to all our prayers. If you pray and ask God to give you a car while you are wasting your money on other things, or to give you an A on your test even though you didn't study for it, God won't answer those selfish prayers. Your prayers are heard, but this doesn't necessarily mean that all of your "desires" will be granted. The true God of the Bible is different from other gods who claim to give everyone exactly what they desire. God won't always answer with a yes. Your motivation needs to be right. Here are three suggestions of how to offer our prayers to God;

a) When praying to God you must pray in the name of Jesus. The first two ways to pray above (in 1: Attitude When Praying) are not a recommendation. They are commands.

John 14:13

"And I will do whatever you ask in my name, so that the Son may bring glory to the Father."

g) ありのままをかくさず祈る（マタイ 6:8）

神様は、あなたのすべてをご存知です。問題も不安も、疑いもすべてです。きれいな口調で祈る必要はありません。神様に身をゆだねて、感じることをすべて祈ってみましょう。神様に正直になると、自分の弱さを受け入れ、問題をゆだねていく事ができます。そのような祈りの中で、あなた自身が気づかされ、また新たに語られることがあるはずです。

h) 具体的に祈る（ピリピ 4:6、第一ペテロ 5:8）

神様はすべてご存知でも、あなたが具体的に祈る時、一つひとつを神様に信頼してゆだねている姿勢を示します。具体的に祈ると、祈りの答えが明確にわかってきます。

i) 一人で祈る（マタイ 6:6）

救われたあなたは、神様と個人的な関係を持っています。一人で静まって、神様の前に出る時間を大切にしましょう。神様はあなたとの時間を嬉しく思っています。

j) グループで祈る（マタイ 18:20）

クリスチャンの兄弟姉妹と共に、祈りを通して神様の前に出ていくのはとても素晴らしい事です。神様の家族としての一致と喜びが深まります。互いのために祈ると愛が生まれてきます。人に祈ってもらうと励ましを受けます。イエス様の名前によって集まる所には、神様もその中にいて下さいます。

2: 祈る際の注意点

神様が祈りを聞いて下さるという真実は、聖書から疑いもなくわかります。しかし、お金を無駄使いしながら「車をください」、勉強せずに「100点がとれますように」というような祈りは、自己中心の願いであり、答えられないかもしれません。ここで「祈りが聞かれる」という時、必ずしも「お願い事が叶う」という意味ではありません。聖書が語る真実の神様は、人間が自分の手に入れたい生き方のために利用するご利益宗教の神々ではないからです。祈りが、答えに導かれるにはいくつかの条件があります。

a) イエス・キリストの御名によって、父なる神様に祈らなければならない。
　　上記の 1: 祈る態度、a)と b)は単なる祈りの目安ではなく、条件です。

ヨハネ 14:13

「またわたしは、あなたがたがわたしの名によって求めることは何でも、それをしましょう。父が子によって栄光をお受けになるためです。」

We pray in the name of Jesus because He reconciled our relationship with God by dying on the cross. We cannot be connected to God without Jesus, because He is a mediator between God and us. Praying in the name of Jesus Christ means that your prayers (such as those of worship, confession of sins, thanksgiving, and personal requests) are accepted only through Christ. This also means that you believe in Christ's deity and trust Christ Himself.

The Gospel of John says that when we pray in the name of Jesus and when the prayers are answered, you personally experience how gracious He is revealing God's glory to us. When prayers are not answered in the way we request, we need to realize that He is sovereign over everything and has a better plan for us. Even when your own personal desires aren't fulfilled, know that God is sovereign over all things. Believe that the Lord has your best interests in mind, according to God's word.

   b) We all must remain in Christ.

John 15: 7

"If you remain in me and my words remain in you, ask whatever you wish, and it will be given unto you."

What a generous promise! Whatever you ask for, God will provide for you as long as you abide in Him. You can do this by making Christ the number one priority in your life and by living your life according to the word of God.

   c) The content of your prayers must be according to His will.

I John 5:14-15

"This is the confidence we have in approaching God: that if we ask anything according to His will, He hears us. And if we know that he hears us - whatever we ask- we know that we have what we asked of him."

We will learn more about the will of God in Step 8 and 9. It is important for us to seek the will of God in order to please Him, rather than to seek personal gain. We need to be careful to examine our motivation in prayer. Let's strive to have God's perspective by nurturing 'the mind of Christ'. Through a personal relationship with Christ, your prayers are heard and answered according to God's will.

イエス様の御名によって祈るのは、あなたがイエス様の十字架によってゆるされ、神様との交わりが修復されたからです。ですから仲介者であるイエス様なしには、あなたは神様に近づくことすらできないのです。イエス・キリストの名によって祈る、とは大切な意味があります。あなたが捧げる祈り（礼拝、罪の告白、感謝、願い事、とりなし等）は、イエス様を通して初めて受け入れられるものです。子として遣わされたイエス・キリストの神性を認め、イエス様ご自身に信頼をおいているという意味も含まれています。

そして、このヨハネの聖句にあるように、祈りがイエス様の御名によって捧げられると、それが答えられた時、神様がどれほど素晴らしく恵み深いお方であるか（栄光が現される）体験できます。それは、あなたが神様をよりよく知っていくプロセスなのです。結果がもともとの自分の願いどうりにならなくても、神様がすべての物事を治めておられる方であると知り、あなたに最善の道をご用意されていることが御言葉によって理解できます。

   b) キリストにつながっていなければならない。

📖 ヨハネ 15:7

> 「あなたがたがわたしにとどまり、わたしのことばがあなたがたにとどまるなら、何でもあなたがたのほしいものを求めなさい。そうすれば、あなたがたのためにそれがかなえられます。」

なんと寛容な約束でしょう！何でも願ってよいのです。ただし「イエス様にとどまっている」事が条件です。イエス様にとどまるとは、生活の中で神様を第一とし、御言葉に従い、みこころを求め、行う努力をする事です。何でも願ってよいのですが、イエス様につながっているならば、自然に、祈りの内容も自分勝手なものになるはずがないのです。

   c) 祈りの内容は、みこころに沿うものでなければならない。

📖 第一ヨハネ 5:14-15

> 「何事でも神のみこころにかなう願いをするなら、神はその願いを聞いてくださるということ、これこそ、神に対する私たちの確信です。私たちの願う事を神が聞いてくださると知れば、神に願ったその事は、すでにかなえられたと知るのです。」

神のみこころについては、Step 8 と 9 で学びます。自分の利益ではなく、神様の願いと目的を果たすためにどのような歩みをするべきか、みこころを求める信仰は神に喜ばれます。祈る時も、そのような純粋な動機が大切です。「キリストの心」を育て（ピリピ 4:8）、あなたが願う事柄が、神様の思いと一致していくように求めましょう。イエス様との関係の中で、祈りは聞かれ、育まれ、みこころに沿って答えられていくのです。

3: The Model Prayer – The Lord's Prayer

This is the Lord's Prayer as Jesus taught it to His disciples. The Lord's Prayer is your model for praying. This doesn't mean praying the exact same prayer; your prayers should include the same ideas.

Matthew 6:9-13

> *"This, then, is how you should pray: Our Father in heaven, hallowed be your name, your kingdom come, your will be done, on earth as it is in heaven. Give us today our daily bread. And forgive us our debts, as we also have forgiven our debtors. And lead us not into temptation, but deliver us from the evil one."*

- "Our father in heaven" teaches to whom your prayers should be directed. It's a prayer focused towards the God of creation who is also the Father of all people.
- "Hallowed be your name" reminds us to respect and honor His name, and tells us to praise Him for who He is.
- "Your kingdom come, on earth as it is in heaven" means that the focus of your prayers isn't on your own desires, but on the accomplishment of God's will.
- "Give us today our daily bread" means to pray that God would meet your daily needs.
- "Forgive us our debts, as we also have forgiven our debtors" means confessing your sins to God who first forgave you, and then forgive others around you.
- "Lead us not into temptation but deliver us from the evil one" means praying that you would not be overcome by sin, and that you would be protected from Satan's attacks.

Summary

Praying to God and spending time with Him will give you understanding from God's perspective. We should remember that praying is essential for us. A conversational prayer is not one sided. It is a conversation between you and God in which you not only talk but also listen. Let's be still and listen as the Holy Spirit speaks to you. Be aware of the communication with God and enjoy the relationship with Him. Let's live this life with the joy of salvation! Let's value our prayer time and enjoy fellowship with God.

Father God, please teach me how to pray. Please send the Holy Spirit to guide my prayers. Help me lift up my prayers individually with thanksgiving. In the name of Jesus I pray, Amen.

3: 祈りの模範 − 主の祈り −

主の祈りとは、イエス様が弟子達に教えられた、模範となる祈りです。これは、一語一句このように祈らなければいけない、という意味ではなく、祈りに含まれるべき内容を教えています。

マタイ 6:9 − 13

「だからこう祈りなさい。『天にいます私たちの父よ。御名があがめられますように。御国が来ますように。みこころが天で行われるように地でも行われますように。私たちの日ごとの糧をきょうもお与えください。私たちの負い目をお赦しください。私たちも、私たちに負い目のある人たちを赦しました。私たちを試みに会わせないで、悪からお救いください。』」

- 「天にいます私たちの父よ。」：誰に向けて祈るのかを教えています。被造物の父、又、信じる者達すべての父である神様に対して祈ります。
- 「御名があがめられますように。」：神様を礼拝し、神様がどういうお方かを賛美します。
- 「御国が来ますように。みこころが天で行われるように地でも行なわれますように。」：自分の願い事を中心にするのではなく、神様のみこころが成されるようにと祈るべきです。
- 「私たちの日ごとの糧をきょうもお与えください。」：あなたの必要を神様が満たして下さるように信頼して祈ります。
- 「私たちの負い目をお赦しください。私たちも、私たちに負い目のある人を赦しました。」：神様に自分の罪を告白し、神様がまずゆるして下さったので、あなたも周りの人をゆるすべきです。
- 「私たちを試みに会わせないで、悪からお救いください。」：罪に打ち勝つための助けとサタンの攻撃からの守りを願います。

まとめのことば

祈れば祈るほど、神様ご自身について、また神様の視点で、物事を見れるようになるでしょう。会話である「祈り」とは、一歩的な申し立てでなく「聞く事」も含まれます。心と霊を静め、あなたの内に宿る聖霊の働きに聞いてみましょう。神様とのコミュニケーションを大切にして、神様との関係を楽しみ、救いの喜びを持って生活しましょう！祈る時間を大切にして、神様との関係を楽しみ、育んでいきましょう。

恵み深い神様、私に祈り方を教えて下さい。聖霊が私の祈りを導いて下さい。あなたに一つひとつの願いを、感謝を、罪の告白を、祈りをもって捧げれるように整えて下さい。アーメン。

Step 7 Sin and Temptation

Now that you have become a Christian, you have a personal relationship with God. However, there is still an unceasing battle against sin and temptation. Know that when you sin against a perfect and holy God, you will never lose your salvation. You could say that a Christian's life is one of continually returning to God. Even though God utterly abhors our sin, don't forget that he always loves us, no matter what.

1: The difference between sin and temptation

Temptation is a challenge from tricking us into committing sin. Satan uses every means possible to pull us away from God, and he delights in our sorrow and failure. However, it is when we are defeated by this temptation that we have sinned. So sin is the result of defeat from the influence of temptation.
Encountering sin is something we face every day. Even Jesus encountered temptation (Luke 4:1-13). However, Jesus never gave in to this temptation and never sinned (Hebrew 4:21).

2: Dealing with Temptation

The areas in which someone is vulnerable to sin or is easily tempted vary from person to person (James 1:14). For one person, it might be alcohol and smoking, and for another it might be sexual sin. It is important not to cultivate the seeds of temptation. For example, if you can't stop smoking, make a concerted effort to stop and don't leave cigarettes lying around. (Colossians 3:5)

- Pray and ask for help! When you are confronted with temptation, you should pray for God to help right away (Hebrews 2:18, 4:16).
- Read the Bible and take refuge in God's word to know how you should think and what you should do (Psalm 119:9,11).
- Be invigorated by knowing Jesus and don't be weighed down by earthly things (Philippians 3:13-14, 4:4-8).
- Pray that you will follow God's teachings and persevere. When you follow God, you will grow closer to him (James 4:8-8).
- Grow in your relationships with other Christians! While encouraging one another, you'll be spiritually strengthened (Hebrews 10:24-25).

With the knowledge of God's truth, you will be able to effectively overcome temptation. By prayer, God's word, and the right thoughts, you will be able to defend against yielding into temptation. Another fruit of being a Christian is self-control. In order to exhibit self-control, let's try out the things listed above!

Step 7 罪と誘惑

あなたもクリスチャンになって、神様との個人的な関係を持てるようになりました。しかし、そこで絶えず起こってくるのが、誘惑、そして罪との戦いです。罪を犯しても救いは決して失わないことを覚えておいて下さい。**罪を犯すとき、完全に聖い神様との交わりが絶たれてしまう**のです。クリスチャン生活とは、神様との交わりに絶えず戻りつづける生活とも言えるでしょう。また、神様は、あなたの罪を非常に嫌われますが、あなたをいつも変わらず愛して下さっているということを忘れないで下さい。

1: 罪と誘惑の違い

誘惑とはサタンによる惑わしです。それは、あなたを罪に落とし入れようとするものです。サタンとは、ありとあらゆる方法を使って、あなたを神様から引き離そうとし、あなたの不幸や失敗を喜びます。そして、あなたがその誘惑に負ける時、罪を犯すのです。ですから、罪とは、誘惑にさらされ、それに負けた時の結果とも言えます。

誘惑にあうのは日常茶飯事です。イエス様も誘惑にあわれました（ルカ 4:1-13）。しかし、イエス様は決して、その誘惑に陥らず、罪を犯しませんでした（ヘブル 4:12）。

2: 誘惑の取り扱い

人によって、弱い部分、誘惑されやすい部分が違うでしょう（ヤコブ 1:14）。ある人にとっては、アルコールやたばこ、他の人にとっては性的な問題かもしれません。誘惑の種を作らない工夫が大切です。たばこを辞められないなら、身の周りにたばこを置かないなど、具体的に努力できることもたくさんあるでしょう（コロサイ 3:5）。

- 祈り、助けを求めましょう！誘惑に直面した時は、すぐに神様に助けを求めるべきです。（ヘブル 2:18、4:15-16）
- 聖書を読み、御言葉をたくわえましょう！考えるべきこと、するべきことがわかります。（詩篇 119:9、11）
- イエス様を知ることに熱中しましょう！この世の重要でない事柄に惑わされなくなります。（ピリピ 3:13-14、4:4-8）
- 神様の教えを守れるよう祈り、努力しましょう！神様に従う時、神様の近くに引き寄せられます。（ヤコブ 4:8-8）
- 神様のために時間を使いましょう！神様の働きを体験できます。（ローマ 12:1-2）
- 他のクリスチャンとの交わりを深めましょう！励まし合いながら、霊的に強められます。（ヘブル 10:24-25）

これらの事項は、誘惑に打ち勝つために有効的です。誘惑に会ったとしても、祈りによって、御言葉によって、又、正しい思いを持つことによって、それに陥る道を防げるからです。クリスチャンとして結ぶ実の一つは自制です。自制できるように、上の事項を試していきましょう。

📖 **Galatians 5:22-23**

"But the fruit of the Spirit is love, joy, peace, patience, kindness, goodness, faithfulness, gentleness, and self-control."

3: Sin and Living by the Spirit

📖 **Romans 8:10**

"But if Christ is in you, your body is dead because of sin, yet your spirit is alive because of righteousness."

📖 **Romans 8:13**

"For if you live according to the sinful nature, you will die; but if by the Spirit you put to death the misdeeds of the body, you will live."

Everyone has fallen into temptation and sinned. Open to Romans 8 and look at the comparison of following the way of Holy Spirit and being in flesh.

- Those who are in Christ are forgiven of their sins and can live filled with the Holy Spirit (vv. 1-3).
- If you are led by the Holy Spirit, you can follow God's law (v. 4).
- In God's eyes, there are clear differences between those who walk in sin and those who walk in the Spirit (vv. 5-8).
- If you live according to sin, you are separated from God (v. 9).
- If you live in Christ, you live according to the Spirit (v. 10).

When you continue to live according to your sin nature, you grow farther and farther from God and persist in a way of life that cannot receive the blessings God has prepared for you. Of course, God does not delight in you when you live in such an unfaithful way.

Jesus has already achieved victory over sin. This means that you, who have placed your faith in Christ, receive the power to overcome sin. Be confident that God has already promised you a victorious life (I Corinthians 15:56-58, Romans 6:11).

📖 **ガラテヤ 5:22-23**
> 「御霊の実は、愛、喜び、平安、寛容、親切、善意、誠実、柔和、<u>自制</u>です。」

3: 罪の葛藤と霊に生きることの原理

📖 **ローマ書 8:10（リビングバイブル）**
> 「キリストがうちに住んでおられるとしても、あなたがたの体は、やはり罪のために死にます。しかし、あなたがたの霊は生きるのです。キリストがあなたがたの霊を赦して下さったからです。」

📖 **ローマ 8:13**
> 「もし古い罪深い性質に従い続けるなら、道に迷い、やがて滅びるしかありません。しかし、もし聖霊様の力によって、その罪深い性質と、邪悪な行いとを打ち砕くなら、あなたがたは生きるのです。」

誰にでも、誘惑に負けて罪を犯してしまう時があります。ローマ書8章をあけてください。クリスチャンが持てる聖霊との歩みと、それを拒否する罪の状態を見てみましょう。

- キリストにあって罪を赦された者は、いのちの御霊に満ちた生活を送れます。（1-3節）
- 御霊に導かれて歩むなら、神様の教えを守れます。（4節）
- 神様の目に、罪に陥って歩む人と、霊によって歩む人には、明らかな違いがあります。（5-8節）
- 罪によって生きるなら、神様から離れています。（9節）
- キリストと共に生きるなら、霊が生きています。（10節）

罪の性質に従い続けて歩んでいると、神様から離れ、神様があなたに用意しておられる祝福を受けずに人生を過ごしてしまいます。もちろん、そのような不信仰の人生を神様は喜ばれません。

イエス様は、罪に対してすでに勝利しているという事実、そしてイエス様にある信仰を得ているあなたにも、罪に打ち勝つ力が与えられている、という真理を覚えていて下さい。あなたも勝利の人生を歩むために、すでに与えられている御言葉の約束を確信して下さい。（第一コリント 15:56-58、ローマ 6:11）

4: Dealing with Sin

a) Let's confess our sins!

When we sin, we grow apart from our relationship to God, so it's necessary to return to a close relationship with Him.

I John 1:9

"If we confess our sins, he is faithful and just and will forgive us our sins and purify us from all unrighteousness."

(Also look at verses 8,10, and Psalm 32.)

God is of course not pleased when we sin, but if we have a proud heart and do not confess our sins it will only lead to more sadness. Constantly sinning intrudes on a great relationship with God, so let's be careful and immediately confess our sins so we can return to a relationship filled with God's grace.

b) Don't rely on your emotions.

Just because we confess our sins and the Bible says that God will forgive us, it doesn't mean that we will feel this way. Even if you confess your sins, it is all too easy to think things like, "I wonder if God is still angry with me?" or "I'm such an awful person." We are subject to ever-changing emotions, but God's truth is eternal. Let's rely on God's word and not our own emotions. You are already forgiven!

Hebrews 10:22-23

"Let us draw near to God with a sincere heart in full assurance of faith, having our hearts sprinkled to cleanse us from a guilty conscience and having our bodies washed with pure water. Let us hold unswervingly to the hope we profess, for he who promised is faithful."

Summary

Christian living is a battle against sin. Even if you sin, you don't lose your salvation but are separated from God in your relationship with Him. Released from our past sins by the forgiveness of the cross, now we have the conviction to walk in God's holiness. Practicing what you've learned from this lesson may be difficult, so pray to be filled and led by the Holy Spirit.

Lord Jesus, who broke the power of sin, please give me the will not to be overcome by temptation. If I sin, help me to confess it right away and return to You. And I pray that I will stay in Your spirit and live according to Your word and not my emotions. Amen.

4: 罪の取り扱い

a) 罪を告白しよう！

罪を犯してしまった場合、神様との交わりが絶たれた状態なので、親しい交わりに戻る必要があります。

第一ヨハネ 1:9

「もし、私たちが自分の罪を言い表すなら、神は真実で正しい方ですから、その罪を赦し、すべての悪から私たちをきよめてくださいます。」

—8節から10節、又、詩篇32篇もみてみましょう。

神様はあなたが罪を犯す時にもちろん悲しまれますが、その罪を正直に言いあらわさず、高慢な心を持っている事にこそとても悲しんでおられます。人は罪を絶えず犯してしまう存在であり、罪は神様とあなたのすばらしい関係の中に入って邪魔をしてしまうものです。罪を犯したと気がつけば、すぐに罪を言い表し、また神様との恵みに満ちた交わりに戻りましょう。

b) 感情に頼ってはいけません。

罪を告白しても、また、聖書に「神様に赦されている」とあるのに、そのように感じない時もあるでしょう。告白しても、「神様怒ってないかな」「自分はだめな人間だ」などと思ってしまうものです。人間の感情は揺れ動くものですが、聖書の真実は永遠に変わりません。自分の感情ではなく、神様の御言葉に信頼しましょう。あなたはすでに赦されていると御言葉は語っています。

ヘブル 10:22-23

「私たちは、心に血の注ぎを受けて邪悪な良心をきよめられ、からだをきよい水であらわれたのですから、全き信仰をもって、真心から神に近づこうではありませんか。約束された方は真実な方ですから、私たちは動揺しないで、しっかりと希望を告白しようではありませんか。」

まとめのことば

クリスチャン生活は罪との戦いです。あなたが罪を犯しても救いは失いませんが、神様との交わりは断たれてしまいます。十字架の赦しによって、過去、現在、そして将来の罪までからも解き放たれ、今、神様の聖さの中にいることを確信しましょう。その確信と信仰、また与えられる平安によって、喜びと希望に満ちた人生を送れるのです。この Step 8 の内容は、理解するのも実践して行くことも一生涯にわたる課題かもしれませんが、今、御霊に満たされて歩めるように祈りましょう。

死の力を打ち破られたイエス様、どうぞ誘惑に負けない力と意思を与えて下さい。もし罪を犯してしまったら、すぐに告白して神様のもとに戻る事ができるように助けて下さい。御霊が私の中に留まり、感情に頼らず、御言葉を信頼して生活できますように。アーメン。

Step 8 Understanding God's Will

There are three aspects of God's will. First, some things, such as Jesus' death on the cross, were deliberately decided and ordained by God. Second, God's will includes things God desires for us to do. Third, there are things such as war and disease that are not caused by God, but which He allows to happen. God also allows people to sin and exercise free will. However, the first and second aspects are God's will and are best for us. As human beings, we try in our actions to rely on all of our experiences and knowledge, but God's way is superior and holds the best things for you. Like the saying "Our way is better, but His way is best!", you will receive His greatest blessings when living a life of knowing and doing God's will.

In the next lesson we will learn specifically how to know God's will, but in this lesson we will start by looking at what exactly God's will is.

1: Things God has already planned (Absolute will)

Isaiah 46:9, 10

"Remember the former things, those of long ago; I am God, and there is no other; I am God, and there is none like me. I make known the end from the beginning, from ancient times, what is still to come."

To begin, we cannot argue with the plans God has already made. We learn about God's acts from the Bible: the creation of the world and mankind, the birth and death of Jesus, the coming new world, judgment after our death, and so on. There are also many times in our lives when God leads us to encounter certain people and situations that are also part of His purposes. These are related to God's absolute purposes, and God is in absolute control of these things, regardless of our desires and choices.

2: Things God desires (such as spiritual growth and morality)

The Bible clearly teaches about God's will in living to please Him. No matter what we believe or how we live, God's desires for us are clearly expressed in the Bible. It's important to take these things to heart in order to live in a way that pleases God so that we will be welcomed in God's kingdom (Matthew 8:21).

Step 8 神のみこころとは

神様のみこころとは、一番目に、イエス様が十字架に架けられたことのように「神様が予め意図されていた計画」、二番目に、「あなたにこうあってほしいと神様が望まれていること」、三番目に、戦争のように神様が起こした出来事ではないが「起こることを許しておられる出来事」などです。三番目のように神様が許容しておられる出来事は、人間の罪や自分勝手な行い故に起こることですが、一番目と二番目のみこころは、あなたにとって最善のものです。人間はあらゆる経験や知識を使って、こうした方がいいという意見や歩み方を持ちますが、神様の方法・道はそれにもまさって最高に素晴らしいものなのです。御言葉を通して神様が何を望んでおられるのかを知り、そのみこころにかなった生き方をすることこそ、神様に喜ばれ、またあなた自身も最高の祝福を受けながら歩んでいけるのです。

次の Step 9 で、具体的にどのように神様のみこころを知れるのかを学びますが、ここではまず、神様のみこころがどのようなものか見て行きましょう。

1: 神様がすでに計画しておられる事（絶対的な意思）

> **イザヤ 46:9、11**
> 「わたしが神である。ほかにはいない。わたしのような神はいない。
> 〜わたしが語ると、すぐそれを行い、わたしが計ると、すぐそれをする。」

まず初めに、神様がすでに決めておられた計画に関しては、議論の余地がありません。聖書から様々な神様の御業が学べます。この世の創造、人類の始まり、救い主の誕生、キリストの死、新しい天地が造られること、人間には死後のさばきがあることなどたくさんあげられるでしょう。あなたの人生においても、神様が特別に出会わせて下さった人や置かれている環境なども、神様のご計画、ご意思のうちにあることが多くあります。これらの、神様の絶対的な意思に関しては、あなたの願望や選択に関わらず、神様が主導権を握って事を成されていくのです。

2: 神様が望まれている事（霊的な歩みや道徳的な事）

聖書には、あなたの歩み方に対するみこころが書かれています。あなたが何を信じ、どのように行動するべきか、神様が望んでおられる事項が明らかに示されています。これらを心にとめ実践していくことは、神様に喜ばれる人生を送るため、また天の御国にふさわしい者とさせて頂くためにも（マタイ 8:21）とても大切です。

For example, God desires..

- that all people be saved (I Timothy 2:4). → Our salvation glorifies God, and we should seek opportunities to share the Gospel with others.
- that we do not follow the world's ways (Romans 12:2) → walk according to the Holy Spirit, confessing our sins and praying.
- that we love God and love those around us (Mark 12:30,31) → put God first and others before ourselves.
- that we always rejoice and have a thankful heart (I Thessalonians 5:16-18) → we dwell on God's blessings even in difficult circumstances.
- that we do not live like those who are not Christians (II Corinthians 6:14) → avoid   unions such as romantic relationships and marriage with those who are not Christians.

These are just a few examples, but by reading the Bible, you can clearly see the way you should live to glorify God. That's why it is imperative to study the Scripture and learn about God and God's will. At times it isn't clear how to do God's will, so pray that you will be able to live a life that is pleasing to God, which shows your obedience to Him. If you really love God, it shouldn't be a burden to choose what He commands (I John 5:3). You are already filled with the Holy Spirit which gives you the power to handle the things you cannot do in your own strength.

You need to give up control of things and trust in the Lord. When God works in your life, it's not when you are living for yourself. It is when you trust His sovereignty and lift up everything to the Lord. This means that you are obeying His will and are living a life with the attitude of Mary who said, "May your word to me be fulfilled." (Luke 1:38). Please don't forget the importance of 'seeking God's will', 'trusting', and 'obeying'.

3: Situations God allows to happen

Romans 8:28

> "And we know that in all things God works for the good of those who love Him, who have been called according to His purpose."

例えば、

- 神様はすべての人が救われることを望んでおられる（第一テモテ 2:4）→ 私が救われたことも神様は喜ばれている。私も他の人に福音を伝えるべき。
- この世の基準に従ってあゆむべきではない（ローマ 12:2）→ 御霊に満たされて歩むために、罪を告白し、祈りを持つべき。
- 神様を愛し、周りの人も愛するように（マルコ 12:30-31）→ 神様をいつも第一とし、人に対しても自分勝手にふるまうべきではない。
- いつも喜び、感謝の心を持つように（第一テサロニケ 5:16－18）→ 困難な状況にあっても、神様からの祝福を思いおこすべき。
- クリスチャンでない人と同じ生き方をしてはいけない（第二コリント 6:14）→ 霊的な一致が持てないのでクリスチャンでない人との恋愛関係や結婚は避けるべき。

これらの聖書箇所はほんの一例にすぎません。聖書には、他にも神様が願われている、あなたがなすべきことが多く書かれています。だからこそ、聖書を学び、神様について、また神様のみこころについて学ぶ必要があります。明らかに示されている聖書箇所でさえ、みこころを実践できない時もありますが、少しでも神様に喜ばれる選択ができるように祈り求め、神様があなたに望まれている生き方ができるように努めましょう。主なる神様に従っているという姿勢は、行いに現れていきます。神様を心から愛するなら、神様の喜ばれることを選び、神様の戒めを守ることは重荷とならないでしょう（第一ヨハネ 5:3）。あなたの内にすでに聖霊が住まわれています。自分ではできない事をできるようにと、聖霊の「助け」を与えられているのです。

あなたは、自分の人生の主権を主にお委ねする必要があります。神様ご自身があなたの人生を通してみこころを成してくださるのは、自分の意志にとらわれた生き方をしている時ではなく、全能なる主に主権をお渡し、結果を委ねている時です。それがみこころに従順であるという状態であり「どうぞ、あなたのおことばどおり、この身になりますように。」（ルカ 1:38）と主に身を委ねた従順な生き方なのです。「みこころに叶うことを求めていくこと」「委ねること」「従うこと」を意識してみて下さい。

3: 神様が望むことではないが、起こる事を許可されている出来事

📖 **ローマ 8:28**
「神を愛する人々、すなわち、神のご計画に従って召された人々のためには、神がすべてのことを働かせて、益としてくださることを、私たちは知っています。」

These are things that God doesn't necessarily plan or desire to occur. However, God allows these events to happen as part of His larger plan for humanity. Everyone wonders why situations such as war, discrimination, persecution of Christians, and other societal problems occur, as well as bad things that happen on a personal level. God sometimes allows things to happen for your edification or for His glory. Some people blame God, but this evil occurs as a result of human sin and not as a result of God's action.

There are many times when you wonder why God allows these things to happen, but often things that you don't understand at present end up working out for your benefit afterward. Because of God's bigger plan, everything has a purpose and reason. Although you don't always understand the purpose and reason for these occurrences, by entrusting them to the God who governs everything and by praying for guidance you can know what you should do at all times. (Ecclesiastes 12:13-14)

Summary

The Bible clearly states God's absolute will and His will for how you should live your lives. Concerning the minor (but important) decisions, the Bible doesn't say which way you should choose. In regard to the things that are written in the Bible, it's good to pray and make an effort to follow them, but there are some instances where the Bible does not say what kind of decision you should make.

In the next lesson, you will look at how to know God's will about specific decisions.

Lord who governs everything, help me to understand the truth concerning Your will, and also give me the wisdom to discern Your will. Amen.

これらの出来事は、神様が意図的に計画したり望まれたりして起こった訳ではないけれども、人間の罪ゆえに起こってしまう状態が許容されていることを指します。クリスチャンであるため殺されしまう国などもあります。戦争、差別や多くの社会問題、また個人レベルでもなぜこのようなことが起こっているのかと疑問に思う時が誰にでもあります。悲しい出来事も、それを通してあなたが整えられたり、神様の栄光が現れたりする機会として用いられて行きます。ある人は神様を責めます。しかし、これらの悪は人間の罪ゆえに起こっているのであって、神様が主導権を握って意図的に起こされたわけではないのがほとんどのようです。

なぜ神様がゆるされているのかその時はわからないことが多くありますが、後になると神様のみこころに沿って益になっているとわかるのです。神様の意思でない出来事までも、すべては神様の御手の中でゆるされて起こっているのです。神様は全地全能の偉大なお方ですから、すべてに目的と意味を持っておられます。あなたにその出来事の意味がわからないからといって、否定的になるのではなく、すべてのものを治めておられる神様に、主導権を委ね、あなたが今の環境において何をするべきか祈り求めましょう。（伝道者の書 12:13-14）

まとめのことば

Step 8 の 1 にある絶対的な神様のご意思と、2 にある神様があなたに望まれる歩みについて、聖書の中にはっきりと書かれている箇所がたくさんあります。しかし、人生の中での細かい（けれども大切な）決断に関しては、どちらの道へ進むべきか書かれていません。書かれていることに関しては、そのように行えるよう祈りながら努めればよいのですが、何がみこころなのか書かれていないことに関しては、具体的な人生の中での決断に対するみこころを知るために人間の側でもするべきことがいくつかあります。

次に続く Step 9 では、具体的な決断の時にどのように神様のみこころを探っていくのか見てみましょう。

すべてのものを治めておられる偉大な神様、あなたのみこころに関する真理を理解できますように助けて下さい。また、みこころを悟れるように知恵を与えて下さい。アーメン。

Step 9 How to Live in God's Will

📖 II Chronicles 16:9

"For the eyes of the Lord range throughout the earth to strengthen those whose hearts are fully committed to Him."

In the last lesson, we looked at the different aspects of God's will and what the Bible says about them. But when it comes to other choices in our lives - like where to go to school, what kind of job to get, and who to marry – the Bible does not say. In order to live in God's will, we need to seek to have a right heart and learn God's will, as well as following His will already expressed in the Bible.

1: Things necessary for God's will to be revealed

a) Always be in right relationship with God.

If you want to know God's will, it's necessary to draw close to Him and know His thoughts. Recognize sin that hinders your relationship with God and confess it right away.

📖 Psalm 66:18

"If you embrace immorality, God does not listen."

To learn more about dealing with sin, look at Step 8, "Sin and Temptation"

If you abide in Jesus, it's easy for the Holy Spirit to work in you. Through the guidance of the Holy Spirit, you can receive the revelation of God's truth (John 16:13-15).

b) Confidently act on what you already know concerning God's will.

📖 John 14:21

"Whoever has my commands and obeys them, he is the one who loves me. He who loves me will be loved by my Father, and I too will love him and show myself to him."

The Bible already says many things about God's will – such as what we should do, and the kind of attitudes we should have, for example. If you do the things God has said and if you are living in His will, He will reveal the answers you are seeking.

To learn more about God's will in general, look at Step 8, "Understanding God's will?"

Step 9 神のみこころに生きるために

📖 第二歴代誌 16：9
> 「主は、その御目をもって、あまねく全地を見渡し、その心がご自分と全く一つとなっている人々に御力をあらわしてくださるのです。」

Step 8 では、みこころの類別や、聖書に明らかに示されているみこころがあることなどを見てきました。けれども、「どの学校へ行くのか」、「どの仕事をするのか」、「誰と結婚するのか」など人生の中で起こってくる選択については、これがみこころですとはっきり書かれていません。神様のみこころにためには、「みこころに生きる」という状態に身を置き、みこころを正しい心で求め、そして、聖書ですでに示されているみこころには従っていく決断が必要です。

1: みこころが示されるために具体的に必要な事

a) 神様との交わりの中に常にいる

神様のみこころを知るために、神様のそばにいて、神様の思いを知らせて頂く必要があります。神様との関係を妨げる罪に気づいたらすぐに告白しましょう。

📖 詩篇 66:18
> 「もしも私の心にいだく不義があるなら、主は聞き入れてくださらない。」

罪については、Step 8「罪と誘惑」を参照。

イエス様との交わりの中にとどまっているなら、聖霊が働きやすい状態にいれます。聖霊の導きにより、神様の真理が語られ、あなたがそれを受けとることができます。（ヨハネ 16:13-15）

b) すでにみこころとわかっている事を行う

📖 ヨハネ 14:21
> 「わたしの戒めを保ち、それを守る人は、わたしを愛する人です。わたしを愛する人はわたしの父に愛され、わたしもその人を愛し、わたし自身を彼に現します。」

聖書にはすでにたくさんの神様のみこころ —あなたがするべきこと、持つべき態度— が書かれてあります。神様を愛するなら、神様の私たちへの願いを生活の中で実践していくことが大切です。神様がおっしゃることを行っているなら、あなたはみこころの中に生きており、今求めている答えも示されていくでしょう。

みこころについては、Step 8「神のみこころとは」を参照。

c) Abide by God's will.

Even though you know God's will is the best for us, it might go against your own will and way of thinking. For example, if you fail to get accepted at a school you want to attend, other choices might appear instead. Or you may be surrounded by people and things you would rather avoid but which God allows in order to challenge you. When God shows His will, it may be contrary to your own thoughts and expectations, but you accept that God has reasons for this and pray that you will happily follow God's will. Do not persist in your own self-centered way of thinking.

d) Pursue an attitude of waiting for God's will.

The answers we seek might come in a few hours or in many years. God has His time for all things (Ecclesiastes 3), so pray for endurance and wait until God's will is revealed. When you're waiting, it's important to believe and walk in the promises of the Bible that you've already received. If God doesn't seem to reveal anything, try adapting the things mentioned above and think about your situation again.

Ecclesiastes 3:11

"He has made everything beautiful in its time."

2: To what kind of person, does God reveal His will?

Because God's greatest concern is that you know Him and live in His will, questions such as where you should work and what school you should attend are not of the greatest importance. However, God is of course interested in the particulars of your lives, so it is fine to request and entrust these things to God. The Bible says that God shows His will to these kinds of people:

- people who want to know and carry out God's will, who will have pure desire in their hearts. (John 7:17)
- people with humbled hearts. (Psalm 25:9, I Peter 5:6)
- people who put God first and seek His guidance wherever they go. (Proverbs 3:5-6)
- people who do not follow the ways of the world. (Romans 12:2, I John 2:15-16)
- people who abide in Christ and ask according to His name. (John 15:8, 16)

God is a living, active being. He has dramatically changed those people who wish to live according to His will. Be obedient by seeking God's best and entrusting your own needs and desires to Him.

c) みこころに従おうという気持ちを持つ

「神様のみこころが私にとって最善だ」とわかっていても、自分の思いに反した方向がみこころかもしれません。例えば、行きたい学校に受からず、他の道が示されることがあるかもしれません。または避けたいような人や出来事が周りにあるかもしれませんが、神様はあえてその難しいと思われることにチャレンジするようあなたに示されるかもしれません。みこころが示されたのなら、自分の思いや期待に反しても、神様が何か目的をもってそのように導いて下さっていると受け入れ、喜んで「主のみこころなら」と受け入れていけるように祈りましょう。自分勝手な思いに固執してはいけません。

d) みこころが示される時を待つ

数時間で答えが与えられる場合もあれば、何年もかかって答えが与えられる場合もあります。すべてのことには神様の時がありますから（伝道者の書3章）、忍耐を持って祈り、みこころが示されるまで待ちましょう。待っている間も、すでに与えられている聖書の約束を信じて歩むことが大切です。もし、なかなか示されないならば、上の事項に自分が当てはまるかどうか、もう一度考えてみましょう。

伝道者の書 3:11

「神のなさることは、すべて時にかなって美しい。」

2: みこころが示される人とは

神様の最大の関心は、あなたが神様ご自身を知り、共に生きていくことですから、「この会社で働きたい」「この学校に行きたい」というような願いが叶えられることが最も重要なわけではありません。しかしながら、神様は愛するあなたの人生における細かい点においてまで目をとめて下さっていますから、そのような願いも求め、ゆだねてもよいのです。聖書は、神様が以下のような人にみこころを示して下さると語っています。

- みこころを知り、行いたいという純粋な願いを持つ者に（ヨハネ 8:18、第一ペテロ 5:6）
- 貧しい（へりくだる心を持つ）者に（詩篇 25:9）
- 行く所どこへおいても神様を第一とし、導きを求める者に（箴言 3:5-6）
- この世と調子を合わせない者に（ローマ 12:2、第一ヨハネ 2:15-16）
- イエス様にとどまり、イエス様の名によって求める者に（ヨハネ 15:8、16）

神様は生きて働かれるお方です。みこころに沿って生きたいと願っている人を劇的に変えて下さるお方です。自分の必要と願いをゆだねつつ、神様の「最善」を求め、示されたことに「従順」である行動を起こしていきましょう。

3: Ways God's will is expressed

📖 Ephesians 5:18

"Therefore do not be foolish, but understand what the Lord's will is."

When God's will is evident, you may not need to use all the criteria listed below. However, in order to avoid the mistake of making a decision based on only one way, it's important to judge God's will from different sources. When it's time to make a decision, trust God confidently and seek confirmation through prayer.

a) Through the Bible (Psalm 119:1-5)

Because the Bible is the guidebook for our lives, the things we should know are all written in it. Through the words collected in the Bible, we can judge what choices are biblical. Let's make sure to read the Bible every day.

b) Through the Holy Spirit (I John 2:28)

The Holy Spirit can give strong confirmation and peace in prayer. Because God lives in you through His Holy Spirit, with the witness of the Holy Spirit you can discern God's will. But because we are influenced by our own desires and emotions, we should also consider other ways to know God's will to avoid misunderstanding.

c) Through your circumstances (Psalm 38:5)

If one way is closed to you, it may be the Holy Spirit leading you to a better way. Look at circumstances you can't control and seek God's guidance.

d) Through other Christians (Hebrews 13:8)

Sometimes Christians who have already grown in the Holy Spirit will offer good advice and prayer, helping you pursue God's will. Look for other Christians filled with God's wisdom.

The Spirit will use these means to confirm the truth of your decision. The Spirit works to show you the will of God and then direct your course of action. When you discern God's will, He will give you total peace and assurance. (Isaiah 26:3)

Summary

📖 I John 5:14-15

"This is the confidence we have in approaching God: that if we ask anything according to His will, He hears us. And if we know that he hears us – whatever we ask – we know that we have what we asked of Him."

3: みこころが示される方法

📖 **エペソ 5:18**
「ですから、愚かにならないで、主のみこころは何であるかを、よく悟りなさい。」

みこころが示されるとき、下のすべての方法を通してではないかもしれませんが、一つの方法だけで早合点してしまわないように、様々な角度からみこころを判断する必要があります。決断の際には、心からの従順と識別を持って、祈りの中で確信することが大切です。

a) 聖書を通して（詩篇 119:1-5）

聖書はあなたの人生のガイドブックですから、あなたが知るべきことはすべて書かれています。聖書の言葉を蓄えていくなら、どの選択肢が聖書的か判断することができます。聖書を毎日読みましょう。

b) 祈りを通して（第一ヨハネ 2:28）

祈りの中で強く確信や平安を与えられ、御霊の働きを感じることがあります。あなたの中に神様（聖霊）が住んで下さっているので、御霊からの語りかけでみこころを悟ることができるのです。しかし自分の願望と感情に左右されて、それを聖霊の働きと勘違いすることがないように、他の方法も必ず考慮しましょう。

c) 状況を通して（詩篇 38:5）

みこころでない道が閉ざされる場合や、またみこころならばすべてのステップがうまく導かれる場合などがあります。自分がコントロールできない状況を見て、神様の導きを悟ることもできます。

d) 他のクリスチャンを通して（ヘブル 13:8）

特に、霊的に成長したクリスチャンからは、神様の働きに対して良いアドバイスを与えられたり、祈りを通して、みこころの追求に一緒に関わってもらえます。神様の知恵で満ちているクリスチャンを探しましょう。

このように、聖霊が様々な形で働かれ、あなたに真実を悟らせて下さいます。みこころが示されるのも、またそれをみこころだと悟り受け止めることができるのも、聖霊の働きがあるからこそでしょう。「これがみこころだ」と悟る時、神様からの完全な平安と確信が与えられます。

まとめのことば

📖 **第一ヨハネ 5:14，15**
「何事でも神のみこころにかなう願いをするなら、神はその願いを聞いてくださるということ、これこそ神に対する私たちの確信です。私たちの願う事を神が聞いて下さると知れば、神に願ったその事は、すでにかなえられたと知るのです。」

When your hearts are right, God's will is something that you can understand quite naturally. There are many things that you hope for and desire, but the most important thing is to practice [1: Things necessary for God's will to be revealed]. If you follow this path, you can live a life of rejoicing in God and receiving the true meaning of God's blessings. When you ask for His direction, God takes pleasure in revealing Himself and making His will known.

Lord, who always guides me, please help me to always abide in relationship with You. Please lead me in living a life of rejoicing in You and help me be able to walk in faith according to Your will. Amen.

あなたの心が神様のみこころにかなった状態である時、自然にみこころを悟ることができるようになります。自分の希望や願う道はそれぞれにありますが、一番大切なことは、上記にある、「1: みこころが示されるために具体的に必要なこと」を実践することです。そうすると「みこころにかなった祈り」を捧げれることができます。みこころにかなった歩みは、神様に喜ばれ、本当の意味で、神様の祝福を受ける人生を送れるでしょう。あなたがみこころを第一に求める時、神様は喜んでご自身を、またみこころを示して下さるのです。

いつも私を導いて下さっている神様、どうぞいつも私があなたとの交わりの中に留まっていることができるように助けて下さい。あなたに喜ばれる生活を送れるように導いて下さい。示されたみこころに、信仰をもって歩む事ができますように。アーメン。

Step 10 The Meaning of Trials

I Peter 1:8

"These have come so that your faith – of greater worth than gold, which perishes even though refined by fire – may be proved genuine and may result in praise, glory, and honor when Jesus Christ is revealed."

Just because you've become a Christian doesn't mean that you won't experience problems and trials. But in a life lived with God you can receive the strength to properly deal with difficult times and use them as an opportunity to continue to grow. Your faith is tested through trials.

In our relationships with others, at school, at work, in sickness, in the struggle against sin, or other minor troubles, there are various trials and hardships to be found. God is with you in each of these challenges. He gives you the strength to overcome them, and He has a purpose for the trials in your life. There are four positive responses that can result from trials.

1: You can grow as a Christian.

We tend to rely on ourselves, our friends, and the circumstances surrounding us; we try to save ourselves. Even if you try to surmount these challenges, there are many more things you can't change in your own power. Use the trials faced in your life as a chance to let God take control.

Because God is love, He does not permit trials that we cannot endure. Instead, He provides a way to escape (I Corinthians 10:13) as well as help and protection (Psalm 121).

- Trust in God's plan (Romans 8:28, Proverbs 3:5-6)
- Pray for and seek God's will (Jeremiah 29:11-13)
- Entrust your problems to God (Psalm 38:5, I Peter 5:8)

Applying these verses during times of trials will help you grow as a child of God. You will learn how to walk with Christ and how to cope when faced with challenging circumstances. Without being overwhelmed by your problems and burdens, you will be looking toward God's greatness and compassion. Through trials, let's experience your walk with Christ.

2: You can repent and return to God.

We don't really know why trials happen. But God has a big plan and we may not be able to understand all of it right now. So when faced with trials, we should focus on what kind of attitude we need to have.

Step 10 試練の意味

第一ペテロ 1:8

「あなたがたの信仰の試練は、火で精錬されつつなお朽ちて行く金よりも尊く、イエス・キリストの現れのときに称賛と光栄と栄誉になることがわかります。」

クリスチャンになったからといって、問題や試練がなくなるのではありません。しかし、神様と歩む人生には、困難を正しく対処し、また成長の機会として神様に用いて頂くために、その試練に耐える力が与えられます。試練を通して信仰が試され、成長させられます。

人間関係の中で、職場で、学校で、病気、罪との戦い、または生活の中でのささいなトラブルなど、様々な試練があるでしょう。神様はあなたが歩むその一つひとつの過程で共におられ、乗り越える力を与えて下さいます。そして、神様はあなたの人生の中で起こる試練についても目的を持っておられます。試練には、以下のような意味があると考えられます。

1: 神様の子どもとして成長する。

私たちは、周りの環境、友人、または自分によく頼りがちになります。自分の力で乗り越え、自分自身で自分を救おうとしても、自分の力で変えられないことを経験します。あなたの人生における試練を、神様が働く機会として用いて頂きましょう。

神様は愛のお方ですから、あなたが耐えられないような試練には遭わせないとおっしゃっています。むしろ、脱出の道を備えて下さっています。（第一コリント 10:13）又、助けと守りを与えて下さいます。（詩篇 121）

- 神様の計画に信頼しましょう。（ローマ書 8:28、箴言 3:5-6）
- みこころを祈り求めましょう。（エレミヤ 29:11-13）
- 問題を神様にゆだねましょう。（詩篇 38:5、第一ペテロ 5:8）

試練の中で、これらの御言葉を実践していくなら、神様の子どもとして成長していきます。問題や重荷に押しつぶされるのではなく、神様の素晴らしさと憐れみを見上げるようになります。試練を通しても、あなたの主であるキリストと共に歩むことを体験していきましょう。

2: 悔い改めて、神様のもとへ立ち返る。

私たちには、すべての試練がなぜ起こるのかを理解できません。しかし、そこに大いなる神様の計画があります。そのすべてを理解することは出来ませんが、試練に遭った時、どのような態度で立ち向かうかに焦点をあてて歩んでいきましょう。

One reason trials occur is to serve as discipline from God. If you continue in a sinful life separated from God, He may use hardships as a way to bring you back to Him.

📖 Hebrews 12:8

"Endure hardship as discipline; God is treating you as sons. For what son is not disciplined by his father?"

(Also, see verse 5 and 6)

📖 Hebrews 12:10-11

"… but God disciplines us for our good, that we may share in His holiness. No discipline seems pleasant at the time, but painful. Later on, however, it produces a harvest of righteousness and peace for those who have been trained by it."

The discipline the Bible teaches is not, as the Japanese worldview suggests, punishment from God. Don't forget about God's love; God always desires the best for you (Jeremiah 29:11-13). It's necessary to resolve problems relating to trials. It's difficult to discern His will if you are separated from God. When trials occur, it's important to always place your relationship with God first, to determine if the trials are God's discipline for you. (I John 1:9)

3: You can become more like Christ.

Another result of trials is sanctification, or becoming more like Christ. By becoming more like Christ, you will love others, follow God's will, and develop your character to more reflect the fruit of Spirit. The process of sanctification continues throughout our lives. God uses the struggles you face to mold you into Christ's image. You become sanctified and refined by maintaining to your faith through the many trials you face in a world ruled by sin.

📖 Philippians 1:29

"For it has been granted to you on behalf of Christ not only to believe on Him, but also to suffer for Him."

一つの試練の理由は、神様からの「懲らしめ」という訓練です。神様から離れ罪深い生活を続けていると、あなたを神様の元へ戻すため、「懲らしめ」という方法で試練を用いる時もあります。

ヘブル 12:8
「訓練と思って耐え忍びなさい。神はあなたがたを子として扱っておられるのです。

「父が懲らしめることをしない子がいるでしょうか。」－5、6節も参照

ヘブル 12:10-11
「。。。霊の父は、私たちの益のため、私たちをご自分の聖さにあずからせようとして、懲らしめるのです。すべての懲らしめは、そのときは喜ばしいものではなく、かえって悲しく思われるものですが、後になると、これによって訓練された人々に平安な義の実を結ばせます。」

聖書が教える懲らしめとは、日本人が持つ価値観の「神からの罰」ではありません。神様は愛である事を忘れないで下さい。神様はあなたへの最善をいつも願っておられます（エレミヤ 29：11－13）。試練に対する問題解決が必要な時、あなたが神様から離れた状態にいるなら、みこころが示されていくことは難しいです。何かの試練ある状況において、その試練が悔い改めを導く懲らしめなのか、訓練のための困難なのかはわかりませんが、どんな困難な中にあっても、いつも神様との交わりを第一にしましょう。(第一ヨハネ 1:9)

3: キリストに似た者へと変えられる。

「イエス様のように変えられるため」に試練は用いられます。イエス様のようになるとは、愛の人になり（神様を愛し、人を愛す）、神様のみこころに従い、また御霊の実を結ぶ人格が整えられることです。これは生涯を通して成されていく御業で、あなたがキリストに似た者となっていく過程の中で、神様は試練を用いられます。罪によって支配されたこの世の中で、多くの試練が起こりますが、精錬された信仰を持つ成熟した者と変えられていくのです。

ピリピ 1:29
「あなたがたは、キリストのために、キリストを信じる信仰だけでなく、キリストのための苦しみをも賜ったのです。」

In the midst of our own suffering we can experience His comfort, His peace, and His joy. Because He Himself suffered, He is able to help those who are suffering. (Hebrew 2:18) Take the opportunities to continue becoming more and more like Christ by experiencing what He went through.

To learn more about becoming Christ-like, look at Step 15: Becoming more like Christ.

4: You can bring glory to God.

When you grow as a child of God, get closer to Him, and become more Christ-like when you walk through trials, opportunities will arise for you to bring glory to God. You glorify God as others witness your godly reaction to the trails you face.

a) You bring glory to God when you heal from suffering and problems.

In John 9, there is an example of a person who was born blind. Jesus said the blindness was not caused by sin. When the man had faith and entrusted his problem to God, God healed him.

Today, God's act of healing works through a person's having an attitude of faith and entrusting his problems to God, resulting in display of God's glory and magnificence. For this reason, it's necessary to pray and entrust your problems to God.

b) You bring glory to God by persisting through adversity.

God does not always choose to heal or solve your problems. If He does not bring healing from your suffering, He has a reason. Live expectantly trusting He will show you His will through your suffering.

📖 James 1:2-3

"Consider it pure joy, my brothers and sisters, whenever you face trials of many kinds, because you know that the testing of your faith produces perseverance."

c) You bring glory to God by becoming the person that the Lord can use.

People faced with trials and suffering can sympathize with others who are experiencing suffering and worry. As a Christian you would be able to show Jesus' love for them. Through your having suffered, you are able to love, understand, encourage, and comfort others who suffer.

苦しみをあなたが体験する時、その中において、キリストからの慰め、平安、喜びなどを体験させられます。キリストご自身が試みを受けて苦しまれたので、試みを受けている者たちを助けることができます（ヘブル2:18）。キリストご自身を体験し、キリストに似た者に変えられていく機会として、試練をとらえましょう。

キリストに似た者については、Step 15「キリストのように変えられる」を参照。

4: 神様に栄光をお返しする。

試練を通して、あなたが神様の子どもとして成長し、神様に近づけられ、ますますキリストのように変えられていくなら、その姿自体で神様の栄光が現される機会として用いられるでしょう。神様の子どもとしてのあなたの姿、それに加え、試練への解決が神様に栄光を帰すことへとつながるのです。

a) 苦しみへの癒し、問題解決を通して

ヨハネの9章には、生まれつき盲人だった人の例があります。だれも罪を犯したわけではありませんでしたが、「神様の業が現われるため」にその人は盲人だったのです。信仰を持って神様に問題をゆだねると、彼は目が見えるようになったのです。このように実際に癒される、という神様の業、またはその人が信仰を持って神様に問題をゆだね希望に満ちて歩む姿は、神様の栄光を示す機会となります。だからこそ、祈って問題をゆだねる必要があるのです。

b) 忍耐を通して

けれども、神様はいつも癒し、問題を解決されるわけではありません。そのような苦難の状況の中にも、神様がされる事には理由があります。信仰が試される苦しみの間、みこころが何なのか、神様が示してくださることを期待していきましょう。

📖 **ヤコブ 1:2－3**

「私の兄弟たち。さまざまな試練に会うときは、それをこの上もない喜びと思いなさい。信仰が試されると忍耐が生じるということを、あなたがたは知っているからです。」

c) 用いられる者となる事を通して

試練に遭って苦しみを味わった人こそ、他人の苦しみや悩みを共感できるものです。神様の子どもとして、　愛に溢れているイエス様のようになるには、周りの人を愛し、理解し、励まし、慰めを提供することが必要です。

II Corinthians 1:4

> "[God,] who comforts us in all our troubles, so that we can comfort those in any trouble with the comfort we ourselves have received from God."

As a Christian filled with love and able to understand people's feelings, let's allow God to use you. When you face trials and learn from them, you can certainly be used to express God's glory. You are to be used as a child of God who understand people's feelings and are filled with love and comfort. Through trials you experience pain, but God certainly uses these so that you can encourage other people to experience Him.

Summary

There is a purpose and meaning behind a Christian's trials and hardships. Therefore it's not just a painful experience, but also one that has hope. Through the hope you have in Christ, you have the power to get past trials. Take trials as an opportunity for God to act in your life. Have faith and fight back against the trials you face. Not one thing happens that God is unaware of, and isn't part of His plan.

It's also important to understand that even Jesus Himself faced trials and understands the hardships and sadness that you face. He knows your struggles and intervenes on your behalf. (Romans 8:26-28) We will have compassion and receive grace and are permitted to approach God's throne of grace in order to receive assistance when the time comes (Hebrew 4:16).

Romans 5:3-5

> "Not only so, but we also rejoice in our sufferings, because we know that suffering produces perseverance; perseverance, character; and character, hope. And hope does not disappoint us, because God has poured out his love into our hearts by the Holy Spirit, whom he has given us."

Lord Jesus, thank You for always being with me, even in difficult times. Please give me the strength to endure trials. Help me to understand what You are trying to teach me through trials, and help me to have hope in waiting for Your plan. Amen.

📖 **第二コリント 1:4**
> *「神は、どのような苦しみのときにも、私たちを慰めてくださいます。こうして、私たちも、自分自身が神から受ける慰めによって、どのような苦しみの中にいる人をも慰めることができるのです。」*

人の気持ちがわかる、愛と慰めに満ちた神様の子どもにならせて頂きましょう。上記の聖句にあるように、あなたの試練を通しての痛みや様々な体験も、他の人が神様に目を向けるよう励ましていくために、きっと用いられるでしょう。

まとめのことば

クリスチャンの試練や苦しみには、意味と目的があります。ですから、ただ苦しいだけで終わるのではなく、希望があるのです。イエス様にある希望こそ、真の生きる力となります。試練を神様が働く機会として受け止めましょう。信仰を持って立ち向かいましょう。偉大な計画を持っておられる神様が知らない所で起こっている出来事は何一つありません。

又、イエス様ご自身も試みに遭われたために、あなたの苦しみも悲しみもすべて理解して下さっています。今もあなたのことを覚え、とりなして下さっています（ローマ８：26－18）。そして「私たちは、あわれみを受け、また恵みを頂いて、おりにかなった助けを受けるために、大胆に恵みの御座に近づく」（ヘブル 4:16）ことが許されているのです。

📖 **ローマ書 5:3-5**
> *「そればかりでなく、患難さえも喜んでいます。それは、患難が忍耐を生み出し、忍耐が練られた品性を生み出し、練られた品性が希望を生み出すと知っているからです。この希望は失望に終わることがありません。なぜなら、私たちに与えられた聖霊によって、神の愛が私たちの心に注がれているからです。」*

　　イエス様、苦しい時も、あなたがいつも私と共にいて下さり、安らぎを与えて下さっていることをありがとうございます。どうぞ私にも試練に耐える力を与えて下さい。この試練を通して、あなたが私に学ばせようとしておられることを悟り、あなたが持っていて下さるご計画に信頼していけますように。アーメン。

Step 11 Christian Fellowship

Ephesians 4:1-2

> *"As a prisoner for the Lord, then, I urge you to live a life worthy of the calling you have received. Be completely humble and gentle; be patient, bearing with one another in love."*

When you become a Christian, your relationships with other people are split into two types. The first is your relationships with other Christians. This is called fellowship, an indispensable relationship in which you grow together as a family to become more like the Lord. The other type is your relationship to people who haven't become Christians yet. Your relationship to them is also an important part of faithful living. Telling them the message of God's love and witnessing to them is part of God's will. In this lesson, we'll look closely at fellowship and relationships with other Christians. Take a look at the next lesson for more about witnessing.

1: About God's Family

God's family includes of all the people who have received Christ's salvation. (John 1:12) God doesn't say that once you become a Christian you should separate yourself from the world and live an isolated life alone. He says that we should share in joy and suffering (Romans 12:15), do good to all people (Galatians 6:10), and love one another. (I John 4:20-21) Having a special spiritual connection, God's family goes beyond blood relations, nationality, and age differences.

God's greatest will is for you to know Him, love Him, and spend eternity with Him. God uses relationships with other Christians to help you grow in the knowledge of Him. Relationships take time to cultivate and may require a new environment, as attending church and Bible study.

> *To learn more about God's family, look at Step 14 The Importance of Church.*

Place a high priority on your relationships within God's family. If you don't have any relationships with other Christians, actively seek them. (Hebrew 10:24-25)

Ephesians 3:18-19

> *"I pray that you, being rooted and established in love, may have power, together with all the saints, to grasp how wide and long and high and deep is the love of Christ, and to know this love that surpasses knowledge – that you may be filled to the measure of all the fullness of God."*

Step 11 クリスチャンとの交わり

📖 エペソ 4:1-2

「召されたあなたがたは、その召しにふさわしく歩みなさい。謙遜と柔和の限りを尽くし、寛容を示し、愛を持って互いに忍び合い、平和のきずなで結ばれて御霊の一致を熱心に保ちなさい。」

クリスチャンになったあなたにとって、あなたの人間関係は2種類に分けられます。一つは、新生された神様の子達との関係です。これは「交わり」とよばれ、主にあって共に成長していく家族として必要不可欠な関係です。もう一つは、まだクリスチャンでない人達との関係です。彼らとの関係もあなたの信仰生活の中でとても重要なものです。神様の愛のメッセージを伝え、「証すること」は神様のみこころです。この Step 11 では、他のクリスチャンとの関係、「交わり」について見ていきましょう。証については次の Step 12 をご覧下さい。

1: 神様の家族とは

神様の家族とは、イエス様の救いを受け入れ、御霊によって生まれた者達すべてが含まれます（ヨハネ 1:12 3:5-6）。神様は、あなたが救いを受け入れて神様の子どもとなった時、この世から離れて一人で清く生きなさいなどとはおっしゃりませんでした。喜びや悲しみを分かち合い（ローマ 12:15）、お互いに善を尽くし（ガラテヤ 6:10）、互いに愛し合いなさい（第一ヨハネ 4:20-21）と言われました。神様の家族とは、血のつながりや国籍や歳の差を超えた、特別な霊的な関係なのです。

神様の最大のみこころは、あなたが神様を知り、神様を愛し、永遠に神様と共にいる事です。他のクリスチャンとの交わりがないと、神の子として成長し神様を知って行く過程において、難しさを覚えるでしょう。時には、日々の生活の中で、あなた自身が、交わりのために時間をかける努力をし、新しい環境に適応していく努力も必要です（例えば、教会へ行く、聖書の学びに参加する等。

教会については、Step 14 「教会の大切さ」を参照。

与えられている神様の家族との交わりを精一杯大切にして下さい。もし今、交わりが与えられていないのならば、与えられるように祈り求め、積極的に行動をとっていきましょう。（ヘブル 10:24 – 25）

📖 エペソ 3:18-19

「すべての聖徒とともに、その広さ、長さ、高さ、深さがどれほどであるかを理解する力を、持つようになり、人知をはるかに超えたキリストの愛を知ることができますように。こうして、神ご自身の満ち満ちたさまにまで、あなたがたが満たされますように。」

2: The Out-Pouring of God's Love

📖 Isaiah 43:4

> *"Since you are precious and honored in my sight, and because I love you, I will give men in exchange for you, and people in exchange for your life."*

When met with God's truth, we see that we are loved and created by God. Through encountering the true God and His true love, you can discover the meaning and value of your life to God. As a child of God and member of His family, you are loved deeply.

Christians who understand God's love can take it and show love to other people. As someone forgiven by God, you should forgive other people, too. Sometimes, loving and forgiving others can feel very one-sided to you. But no matter how you interact with others, God says to love them – that's what Jesus did. Love is not feeling but a commitment. At times this can be challenging, but we are to show God's love to everyone in God's family. (Gal. 6:9-10, Phil. 2:4)

📖 I John 4:9-11

> *"This is how God showed his love among us: He sent his one and only Son into the world that we might live through him. This is love: not that we loved God, but that he loved us and sent his Son as an atoning sacrifice for our sins."*

3: Unity through the Spirit

In various Bible passages, we are told to love and encourage each other without being judgmental, thereby promoting unity in the body of Christ. The Lord says to love our brothers and sisters in Christ. Although there are situations where Christians can experience love simply because their shared faith, there are also times where it's hard to love each other. In any case, you need to learn God's will revealed in the Word, and putting it into practice while trusting in God. Look at the passage below.

📖 Philippians 2:1-2

> *"If you have any encouragement from being united with Christ, if any comfort from his love, if any fellowship with the Spirit, if any tenderness and compassion, then make my joy complete by being like-minded, having the same love, being one in spirit and purpose."*

2: 注がれている神様の愛

📖 **イザヤ 43:4**

「わたしの目には、あなたは高価で尊い。わたしはあなたを愛している。」

真実の神様に出会い、あなたは愛されて創造された尊い存在であるとわかります。本当の神様、本当の愛を知ったあなたは、人生の意味と価値を神様との生活において見い出すことができたでしょう。あなたは神様の子どもとして、家族として深く深く愛されているのです。

神様の愛を理解しているクリスチャンは、その注がれている愛を持って他の人を愛すことができます。あなたがゆるされている神様からのゆるしを持って、他の人をゆるすことができます。時にはあなたの側から愛し続け、許し続けなければならない一方通行かもしれません。相手の対応がどうであっても、人を愛すことは神様からの命令です。それはイエス様も通られた道です。時には困難な状況もありますが、神様の家族との交わりの中で、その愛を実践することを学ぶのです（ガラテヤ 6:9-10、ピリピ 2:4）。

📖 **第一ヨハネ 4:9-11**

「神はそのひとり子を世に遣わし、その方によって私たちに、いのちを得させてくださいました。ここに、神の愛が私たちに示されたのです。私たちが神を愛したのではなく、神が私たちを愛し、私たちの罪のために、なだめの供え物としての御子を遣わされました。ここに愛があるのです。愛する者たち。神がこれほどまでに私たちを愛してくださったのなら、私たちもまた互いに愛し合うべきです。」

3: 御霊による一致

聖書の様々な箇所に、「互いに愛し合いなさい」「さばき合わずに励まし合いなさい」「一致を保ちなさい」と示された言葉があります。特に信仰の家族を愛するように、とも書かれています。クリスチャン同士だからこそ本物の愛を体験し合うことが出来る場合もあれば、かえって、愛し合うのが難しい場合もあります。いずれにしろ、御言葉によって示されている神様のみこころを学び、神様に拠り頼みつつ愛を実践していく必要があるのです。

📖 **ピリピ 2:1-2**

「もしキリストにあって励ましがあり、愛の慰めがあり、御霊の交わりがあり、愛情とあわれみがあるなら、私の喜びが満たされるように、あなたがたは一致を保ち、同じ愛の心を持ち、心を合わせ、志を一つにしてください。」

Sometimes you might experience problems, but as a companion of Christ and member of God's family, you are indwelled by the Holy Spirit. When you're with other Christians, you can rejoice knowing you share this same special relationship. In spite of human emotions of love and hate, you share a spiritual connection with other believers who know God. If a problem arises with other Christians, entrust your feelings to the Lord and examine your heart. (Matthew 7:1-5) No matter what kind of emotions or problems you face, it's possible to be united – the strength of spiritual union overcomes human strength. If you're truly led by the Spirit of Christ, the same spirit will bring about a match. So if Christians are led by the Spirit and love one another, God will be honored at those times. (John 13:34-35)

Summary

Ephesians 4:1-5

"As a prisoner for the Lord, then, I urge you to live a life worthy of the calling you have received. Be completely humble and gentle; be patient, bearing with one another in love. Make every effort to keep the unity of the Spirit through the bond of peace. There is one body and one Spirit– just as you were called to one hope when you were called – one Lord, one faith, one baptism."

By maintaining and valuing healthy relationships within God's family, you will grow abundantly as a Christian. Seek unity through the Spirit even when problems arise, and try to discover God's desire for you.

Lord of peace, thank You for giving me Your Holy Spirit. Please give me good relationships with other Christians. Please lead me to value fellowship with others, loving and encouraging my brothers and sisters in Christ. Amen.

人間同士はぶつかる時もあります。しかし、救われた者達には、御霊が与えられており、特別な「御霊の交わり」があります。他のクリスチャンと一緒にいる時、御霊の交わりを喜ぶ事ができるでしょう。人間的な好き嫌いの感情があっても、同じ神様を見上げる者達は、御霊でつながっています。愛するとは、感情ではなく意志です。何か問題が起こった時には、まず神様に自分の思いをゆだね、吟味する必要があります。自分の見解や、心を改めるべきだと示される場合もあるでしょう（マタイ７：１－５）。どのような個人的な思いや問題があっても、神様の家族とは一致が可能です。人間の力を超えた、「御霊の一致」がある（あるべき）からです。本当にキリストの御霊に導かれるのなら、同じ御霊によって一致がもたらされます。そして、御霊に導かれ、クリスチャン同士が愛を実践するなら、神様はそのような時にも栄光を受けられます。（ヨハネ 13:34－35）

まとめのみことば

エペソ 4:1－5

「召されたあなたがたは、その召しにふさわしく歩みなさい。謙遜と柔和の限りを尽くし、寛容を示し、愛を持って互いに忍び合い、平和のきずなで結ばれて御霊の一致を熱心に保ちなさい。からだは一つ、御霊は一つです。あなたがたが召されたとき、召しのもたらした望みが一つであったのと同じです。主は一つ、信仰は一つ、バプテスマは一つです。」

神様の家族との豊かな交わりの中で、あなたは神様の子どもとして豊かに成長させられるでしょう。他のクリスチャンとの交わりを大切にしていきましょう。問題が起こる時にも、聖書から神様があなたに望まれていることを学び、御霊の一致を求めましょう。

平和の造り主なる神様、あなたが私達一人ひとりに与えて下さった聖霊をありがとうございます。他のクリスチャンとの良い交わりを与えて下さい。交わりの時間を大切にし、お互いに愛を示し、励まし合えるように導いて下さい。アーメン。

Step 12 The Art of Witnessing

Mark 16:15

"He said to them, 'Go into all the world and preach the good news to all creation."

Witnessing is the act of telling the gospel of Christ to those who have not yet been saved. This includes directly sharing with other people the gospel and grace you have received from God, as well as things like inviting others to church or distributing evangelistic materials as Bibles, tracts, or CDs. The word *witness* is a translation of the Greek *martyria*, which signifies *evidence, attestation of character, reputation*. The emphasis in this commission is on being living evidence of Jesus Christ through the enabling power of the Holy Spirit. Pray others will see Jesus in you!

God guided you to hear the gospel and to receive His salvation, enabling you to have a new walk with God. God may have used someone who shared the Good News with you. Now it is your turn. You are entrusted with praying and sharing the gospel with unsaved friends and family. God can use you to show them the love of Christ, how to have a blessed, fulfilled life on this earth and an eternal destination in heaven.

God will use you when you have a heartfelt desire to share the gospel with others. Some people will never hear the Gospel unless you tell them, but there is a way to share the Gospel that's just right for you! Testify joyfully and confidently about what Jesus did for us.

1: Why should we witness?

a) Witnessing is God's desire

I Timothy 2:4

"God wants all men to be saved and to come to a knowledge of the truth."

God desires for everyone to be saved, and God chose you to be His ambassador. (II Corinthians 5:20) As a Christian, you should have an attitude of willingness for Him to use you to share the gospel. Be willing to offer yourself to God and be available for His purpose to be accomplished. When you have faith and a humble heart, God will use you in a great way to bring about His glory!

Step 12 証人となる素晴らしさ

📖 **マルコ 16:15**

「イエスは彼らにこう言われた。全世界に出て行き、すべての造られた者に、福音を宣べ伝えなさい。」

証人(witness)とは、まだ救われていない人に、キリストの福音を伝えていく人です。直接福音を伝える事も、あなたが受けた神様の恵みを分かち合う事も、教会へクリスチャンのイベントへ誘う事も、聖書やトラクト（福音に関するちらしや小冊子）や伝道メッセージのCDを渡す事も証しする事につながります。ですが一番大切な事は、witnessという言葉の意味が「証拠」「人格による立証」「評判」等であるように、イエス・キリストにある救いの力によってあなた自身が変えられた「証人」として生きることにあります。人々があなたの中にイエス様を見出すように祈りましょう。

あなたが福音を聞き、救われて神様との素晴らしい歩みが与えられたのは、もちろん神様の導きですが、あなたの周りの誰かがあなたにグッドニュース（良き知らせ）を伝えてくれたからでしょう。次はあなたの番です！あなたも、まだ救われていない家族や友達のために祈り、福音を伝えて行く働きがゆだねられています。キリストの愛、この世での恵みにあふれた人生、またその人達が永遠に神様と共にいれるという真理を伝えるために、神様はあなたを用いられます。

人の救いは神様のご計画によるものですが、神様はあなたを他の人の救いのために用いたいと心から願われています。そしてあなたにしか福音を分かち合えない人、あなたにしか分かち合えない方法があるのです！喜びと共に、イエス様があなたに何をして下さったか、証ししていきましょう。

1: なぜ証しするのか

a) 神様の願いなので

📖 **第一テモテ 2:4**

「神は、すべての人が救われて、真理を知るようになるのを望んでおられます。」

すべての人が救われることは、神様ご自身の願いです。そして、神様はあなたを用いるために選ばれました。（第二コリント 5:20）御霊が働かれなければ、誰も福音を信じる事はできません。すべての人が救われる事を神様が願い、そのためにあなたを用いられるのですから、神様が働かれやすいように、あなたも自分自身を主に捧げていく必要があります。神様についていく思いとへりくだった信仰を持つ時、あなたは小さき者でも神様の栄光のために大きく用いられるでしょう！

b) God commands us to witness

II Timothy 4:2

> *"Preach the Word; be prepared in season and out of season; correct, rebuke and encourage – with great patience and careful instruction."*

It is God's will and desire that you proclaim His salvation. If you strive to walk with the Lord, you need to pursue Him and be available to what He wants you to do. (John 8:31)

c) Witnessing bring joy

Because you've experienced God's grace and His work in your life, you will naturally desire to witness to others. You don't witness out of a sense of obligation or desire for others to think well of you.

When you testify about God, the Holy Spirit will guide your speech. Pray for the Spirit to give you the words to say, and then boldly and joyfully share the gospel. When God works through your speech, He is also already working in the hearts of those listening.

In Acts, there are many examples of Christians who witness while filled with joy, affecting the people around them. (Acts 13:16-52)

2: How do I witness to others about God?

a) The information to share

In order to witness, you must understand the problem of sin, man's separation from God, and salvation through Christ. It's not sufficient only to talk about God's existence and about what Jesus taught. You have to show that Jesus settled the problem of our sin through the cross. It is necessary and God's desire for us to repent and change our direction in life.

Of course, your personal experience allows you to share what God and His Holy Spirit are presently doing in people's lives. God's grace is His love and forgiveness at the cross. Have confidence in sharing the good news of the Gospel. Share about your renewed relationship with God through the cross, so that other people can experience God's love and grace, too. (Romans 1:16)

b) 神様からの命令なので

📖 第二テモテ 4:2

「みことばを宣べ伝えなさい。時が良くても悪くてもしっかりやりなさい。
寛容を尽くし、絶えず教えながら、責め、戒め、また勧めなさい。」

あなたが主イエス様の救いを宣べ伝えて行く事は、明らかに神様のみこころであり命令です。命令というと強制的に聞こえますが、もしあなたが本当にイエス様と共に歩んで生きたいと願うなら、神様が言われることに忠実に答えていけるよう努めましょう。（ヨハネ8：31）

c) 証する喜びがあるから

あなたが証するのは、神様の御業や与えられた恵みがあまりに素晴らしいので、他の人に伝えずにはいれないからです。義務感からや、人に良く思われるために神様の話をするのではありません。本当に救いを受け、救いの素晴らしさを体験した者にとって、福音を宣べ伝えることは喜びとなるでしょう。

神様の素晴らしさについて証言する時、あなたが語るべき事さえも聖霊の働きによって与えられるのです。ただ聖霊に、どのように話すべきか祈り求めて、大胆に喜びを伝えたらよいのです。神様があなたの口を通して、聞く者の心にもすでに働いて下さっているのです。使徒の働きには、喜びに満ちた証が用いられ、聖霊の働きによって周りの人達が救われていた例が多く書かれています。（例：使徒の働き 13:16-52）

2: どのように証しするのか

a) 伝える内容

福音を伝える際、まず、唯一の神様の存在や、人間がもともと神様から離れているという罪の問題を理解してもらう必要があります。そして、キリストを通してのみ、救いがある事を伝えます。漠然と、神様の存在への理解や、キリストの教えは素晴らしいと同意するだけでは十分ではありません。十字架を通しての罪の問題の解決を、自分の事として受け入れる必要があります。悔い改め、神様に望まれる生き方に方向転換していくことを促していきましょう。

もちろん、あなたの個人的な体験談は、神様がどのように、実際人々の人生の中で働かれておられるのか、という聖霊の働きの証です。神様の恵みは、十字架での赦しとその愛を受けて、生きたものとなります。福音—グッドニュース—とは、キリストの十字架を通して神様との関係の修復がされた恵みです。神様の愛と恵みを体験できる人生がある事を、自信を持って伝えていきましょう。（ローマ 1:16）

b) The right attitude for witnessing
- **Be humble**
  Witnessing is not conveying that you are a righteous person since you were rescued from sin by God's grace. You are not saving anyone on your own; rather your testimony is joined with God's act of salvation. It is the Holy Spirit who prepares hearts and draws people to the Lord. Even if you have confidence in the truth of the Bible, make sure you always have a humble attitude.
- **Be respectful**
  Even if someone hasn't been saved yet, don't look down on him. God's word says to humbly consider others above yourself. (Philippians 3:3) Do not reject their circumstances and lifestyle. You don't have to be in agreement with them to receive them. Through accepting your friends with love, you can build a relationship of trust with them.
- **Be careful about your speech**
  If you have a heart of humility and respect, the right words will come to you naturally. (Colossians 4:5-6) Do not overwhelm your friend with Christian doctrinal terms, such as atonement, righteousness, holiness, spiritual gifts, or the Holy Spirit which will be difficult for people to understand. Try to look at your witness from your friend's perspective and use words that would be easy for them to understand; in other words, try to remove the misconception that "Christianity has nothing to do with me!" or "Christianity is too complicated!" While considering your partner's perspectives and thoughts, be conscious of avoiding what could cause them to stumble.
- **Make an effort to cultivate good relationships**
  It can be difficult to witness to people who are close to you, as close friends or family members. They are the ones who often know "all" of us, both the good and the ugly. However, in trusted relationship, God can use both your actions and beliefs as a testimony. Even through our weakness, Christ's light shines out to others as a beacon of hope and truth. (Matthew 5:16) God can use any Christian to witness regardless of his age or experience. It doesn't matter if you were just saved today or fifty years ago.

  If you grow as a Christian and bear the fruit of the Spirit in your life, you will influence people around you and cause them to think "I'm drawn to what that person says," "I want to be like that person," "I want to know the God that person believes in, too." When you bear the fruit of the Spirit, such as love, joy, peace, patience, kindness, honesty, gentleness, with an attitude of self-control, you will build good relationships with others. (Galatians 5:22)

b) 証しする際の態度

- **謙遜さを持って**
  福音を分ち合うという事は、救われたあなたが正しい人間である事を証明するのではありません。あなたも神様の恵みゆえに、罪から救われたのです。あなたが誰かを救うのではなく、神様の救いの御業に交えて頂いているのです。神様に人々を近づけるのは、聖霊の働きによります。聖書の真実性に自信があったとしても、決して謙遜な態度を忘れないようにしましょう。

- **尊敬の心を忘れずに**
  相手がまだ救われていないからといって、その人を見下したりしてはいけません。「へりくだって、互いに人を自分よりもすぐれた者と思いなさい」(ピリピ 3:3)という御言葉はクリスチャンでない人たちにも実践しましょう。その人の今まで歩んできた生き方、考え方、状況などを否定するのではなく、受け入れましょう。同意する必要はありません。愛を持って相手を受け入れるなら、信頼ある人間関係が築いていけます。

- **言葉使いに注意する**
  謙虚さや尊敬の心を持っていれば、言葉使いにも自然に現われてくるでしょう（コロサイ 4:4-6）。また、神学的な専門用語（罪の贖い、義化、聖化、賜物、御霊など）は聞き慣れない人にはわかりにくいものです。相手の立場になって、わかりやすい言葉に言い換えて説明しましょう。それは、「キリスト教は自分には関係ない」「聖書は難しすぎる」という偏見を取り除く事にもつながります。相手の立場や考えを配慮しながら、何が「つまずき」であるのかを考え、そのつまずきをもたらさないように気をつけましょう。

- **よい人間関係を作る意識をもつ**
  家族や親友、またその他の親しい人はあなたの良い所も悪い所も知っているために、彼らに証をしていくことの難しさを覚えるでしょう。しかし通常、信頼ある良い人間関係を通してこそ、言葉と態度の両方を持って、素晴らしい証人として用いられます。もちろん、今救われたばかりのクリスチャンもその喜びが良い証となります。年数や経験など関係なく神様は、すべてのクリスチャンを用いられます(マタイ 5:16)。神様の子どもとして成長し、御霊の実があなたの人格の中で作られているのなら、周りの人から尊敬され、「あの人が言ってる事に惹かれる」「あの人のようになりたい」「あの人が信じている神様を私も知ってみたい」と思われるでしょう。愛、喜び、平安、寛容、親切、誠実、柔和、自制などの御霊の実が実っていく中で、良い人間関係も築かれていくでしょう。(ガラテヤ 5:22)

c) With prayers to the Lord

📖 Proverbs 15:29

"The Lord is far from the wicked, but He hears the prayer of the righteous."

📖 I John 5:14-15

"This is the confidence we have in approaching God: that if we ask anything according to His will, He hears us. And if we know that He hears us – whatever we ask – we know that we have what we have asked of Him."

Salvation is obviously God's desire for everyone. However, keep in mind that not everyone who hears the Word will repent and receive salvation. Pray passionately for those with whom you share the Gospel, that their hearts might become open to God. God would use your life. Always be prepared to give an answer to everyone who asks you to give the reason for the hope that you have.

Summary

Salvation is God's work, and your sharing the Gospel is a part of God's great plans. If a friend doesn't accept the Gospel, that's not your fault. Your role is simply to tell them. You share the Gospel and testify to what Christ did for you. Keep praying that you will sow the seeds of the Gospel, grow with God, and bear fruit. Pray that you'll be filled with God's love and be able to boldly proclaim the Gospel.

📖 Romans 10:14

"How, then, can they call one the one they have not believed in? And how can they believe in the One of whom they have not heard? And how can they hear without someone preaching to them?"

🙏 *Lord, please change me according to your Holy Spirit that is in me and all around me that I may be able to boldly proclaim Your Gospel. Please help me exhibit Your grace and magnificence anywhere and everywhere, and place people in my path with whom to proclaim Your Gospel. Amen.*

c) 祈りを持って主にゆだねる

📖 **箴言 15:29**
「主は悪者から遠ざかり、正しい者の祈りを聞かれる。」

📖 **第一ヨハネ 5:14-15**
「何事でも神のみこころにかなう願いをするなら、神はその願いを聞いてくださるということ、これこそ神に対する私たちの確信です。私たちの願う事を神が聞いてくださると知れば、神に願ったその事は、すでにかなえられたと知るのです。」

人が救われる事は、明らかに神様の望みです。しかし、覚えておいて下さい。伝えた相手が、必ずしも全員悔い改めて、救いに至るわけではありません。あなたが福音を分ち合う人が神様に対して心を開く事ができるよう、熱心に祈りましょう。神様はあなたを通して働かれます。いつでもどこにいても、誰に対してでも、神様の証人として用いてもらえるように祈りましょう。（第一ペテロ 3:15）

まとめのことば

救いは神様の御業です。福音を伝えるべきなのは、あなたが神様の大きな働きの中に加えられているからです。もし相手が福音を受け入れなかったとしても、それはあなたの責任ではありません。あなたの役割は、「伝える」ということです。福音を伝え、イエス様があなた自身にして下さった恵みを証することが任されているのです。蒔いた福音の種を、神様が成長させ、実を成らせて下さるように祈り続けましょう。神様からあなたへの愛が、周りにも溢れ出て、福音を大胆に伝えて行く者となれるように祈りましょう。

📖 **ローマ 10:14**
「しかし、信じたことのない方を、どうして呼び求めることができるでしょう。聞いたことのない方を、どうして信じることができるでしょう。宣べ伝える人がなくて、どうして聞くことができるでしょう。」

🙏 私の内で、また周りで働かれる聖霊様、どうぞ大胆にイエス様の福音を語れる者へと変えて下さい。あなたからの恵みを、素晴らしさを、いつでもどこでも証していけますように。私が福音を伝えるべき人を私の前において下さい。アーメン。

Step 13 Serving God

Ephesians 4:11-13

"It was He who gave some to be apostles, some to be prophets, some to be evangelists, and some to be pastors and teachers, to prepare God's people for works of service, so that the body of Christ may be built up until we all reach unity in the faith and in the knowledge of the Son of God and become mature, attaining to the whole measure of the fullness of Christ."

God accomplishes His work through the people that He saves. Having experienced God's love and being filled with His joy, we are entrusted with God's grace and salvation. Serving God isn't just doing something to make Him happy; the reason we serve is to delight in Him and rejoice in living and serving Him. Serving God is not based upon expectation of rewards, or from a sense of duty, guilt, or fear. God has a plan for your life, so discover what God desires for you now.

1: Spiritual Gifts

Spiritual gifts are abilities God gives to all believers to advance His works. In the Scripture, they are categorized into two categories: speaking and serving. Teaching, ministering, exhorting, and leadership fall under the speaking category, while giving and good works come under serving. There may be other types of spiritual gifts as well, such as music, writing, evangelism, encouragement, helping, and hospitality. Each Christian has received gifts "according to the grace given to us". (Romans 12:6)

I Corinthians 12:4-11 says that there are different kinds of gifts and service, but the same Spirit, the same Lord. There are different kinds of ministries, but the same God works all of them. Each one of the spiritual gifts are given for the common good.

Scripture compares the body of Christ to be a human body. The body is composed of many different individual parts. Because all the parts of a body are necessary, the eye shouldn't think it's more important than the hand or the ear, mouth, or foot. (verses 14-31) Each person is important to the body of Christ.

There are many things God allows to happen that we can't do on our own. Without comparing yourself to other Christians or competing with them, you can diligently serve God in the responsibilities He reveals to you.

Step 13 神に仕える

📖 エペソ 4:11-13

「こうして、キリストご自身が、ある人を使徒、ある人を預言者、ある人を伝道者、ある人を牧師また教師として、お立てになったのです。それは、聖徒たちを整えて奉仕の働きをさせ、キリストのからだを建て上げるためであり、ついに、私たちがみな、信仰の一致と神の御子に関する知識の一致とに達し、完全におとなになって、キリストの満ち満ちた身たけにまで達するためです。」

神様は、救われた一人ひとりを用いて、神様の働きを成そうとされます。救われた者達は、偉大な恵みの救いに預かり、神様の愛を経験し、喜びに満たされます。神様に仕えるとは、見返りを期待して働いたり、義務感や罪責感、恐れなどゆえに奉仕をしてすることではありません。神様を愛するゆえ、また神様と生きる人生を喜んでいるゆえ、心からの喜びをもって奉仕することです。ですから、神様があなたの人生に持って下さっているご計画、あなたが今与えられている場でどのように仕える道が示されているのかを見極め、神様があなたの身の周りで起こそうとされている御業に参加しましょう！

1：（霊的）賜物とは

賜物とは、神様の働きを前進させるために、神様がすべてのクリスチャンに与えて下さったものです。おもに、話す事に関する賜物と仕える事に関する賜物の二種類に分けられます。教える事、牧会、指導、励ましなどは、話す事に関する賜物です。他方は、奉仕、慈善、与える事などの賜物です。その他の賜物として、音楽、文才、伝道、手助け、もてなしなど、限りなく挙げられます。すべてのクリスチャンは、それぞれに異なった霊的賜物が「与えられた恵みに従って」与えられています（ローマ 12:6）。

第一コリント 12:4－11 には、賜物、奉仕、働きにはいろいろな種類があること、すべての人の中ですべての働きをなさるのは同じ主であり、同じ神様であること、また、みなの益となるためそれぞれに賜物が与えられている、と書かれています。

また、人間の体を用いて、キリストの体について説明されています。一人ひとりが体の器官であり、一つの体を建て上げるのなら、目が手に向かって「あなたは必要でない」ということはできないし、目も耳も口も手も足も、すべて尊い一つの部分なのです(14－31 節)。一人ひとりがキリストの体にとって重要なのです。

神様はあなただけにしかできないことを与えて下さっています。他のクリスチャンと比べたり競ったりするのではなく、あなたが神様から示されている働きに使命と責任を持って、忠実に仕えていきましょう。

2: Responsibility of using spiritual gifts

The purpose we are given spiritual gifts is written in Ephesians 4:12 - "to prepare God's people for works of service, so that the body of Christ may be built up." As it continues in verse 13, all Christians are called to have faith and grow as part of the body of Christ (the church) by having faith and performing works of service.

Because gifts are abilities given to you by God, it really means to use them to serve the Lord. As a result, you should view it both as a responsibility to use the gifts in your life to serve God, and as a pleasure. First, consider what kind of gifts God has given you. What are your strong points, talents and abilities? What do you enjoy doing? When you are sure of what gifts you possess, the next step is to pray and ask God how you can best use them.

I Corinthians 12:31
"But eagerly desire the greater gifts."

Pray and search for things that you are able to do and for work God desires you to do. In challenging yourself through personal experience, you discover your skills and abilities and find opportunities to use them for God's service.

As you evaluate your gifts, there may be some that you haven't noticed before. In the work of the church and in the lives of other Christians around you, there are many opportunities to advance God's works.

3: Purpose and attitude of serving

Matthew 20:28
"The Son of Man did not come to be served, but to serve, and to give His life as a ransom for many."

2: 賜物を用いる責任

エペソ 4:12 には、賜物が与えられた目的が書かれています。「聖徒たちを整えて奉仕の働きをさせ、キリストのからだを建て上げるため」です。そして、続く 13 節にあるように、信仰が整えられ、奉仕の働きが成され、キリストの体（教会）の成長の一部となっていく事こそ、すべてのクリスチャンに求められているのです。

賜物とは、あなたが神様から授かっている能力ですから、主のために用いてこそ本当の意味があるのです。ですから、与えられている賜物を神様のために用いるのは、あなたの人生に与えられた大きな責任であり、喜びとなるはずです。まず、自分にどのような賜物が与えられているのか、考えてみましょう。何を得意とするのか、どんな能力が与えられているのか、何に喜びを感じるか。賜物を見極めることができたら、次は、どのような形でそれを主のために生かすことができるのか、あなたに対するみこころを祈り求めましょう。

第一コリント 12:31

「あなたがたは、よりすぐれた賜物を熱心に求めなさい。」

「自分には何ができるのか」「何を神様は今自分に求めておられるのか」を祈りながらあなたが仕える道を探し求めてみて下さい。そして、様々な事に挑戦したり体験したりする時、自分が得意とする事や、向いている事、「神様のために、よりよくできるようになりたい」という思いが与えられるかどうかなども発見していきましょう。主の働きのために仕える場や機会も祈り求めてみましょう。

今、あなたの賜物について自己判断できることがあると同時に、あなたのまだ気づいていない賜物がたくさんあるはずです。教会やその他のクリスチャンの働き、周りの人との関係において、神様の働きを前進させるためにできることが数限りなく見い出せるでしょう。

3: 仕える目的と態度

マタイ 20:28

「人の子が来たのが、仕えられるためではなく、かえって仕えるためであり、また、多くの人のための、贖いの代価として、自分のいのちを与えるためであるのと同じです。」

Treat these gifts as a wonderful opportunity to serve God, not as an obligation. Think about God's leading in your life. If you are joyful in your walk with God, the desire to serve Him will come naturally.

One purpose of your life is to serve God by displaying His glory. As a result, the gifts you have are not only for your own use or edification, but are to be used by God.

Summary
God's greatest desire is for people to be saved and grow through the Holy Spirit. Serving God is an essential part of growing as a Christian. When you serve others, you glorify God as you offer yourself to Him and manage the gifts He has given you. You are also learning how to witness to those around you. By your experience and continued increase in knowledge, you are learning about God's character and His desires for your life.

I Corinthians 3:6

"I planted the seed, Apollos watered it, but God made it grow."

The most important thing to remember is to let God control the growth. Therefore, be diligent to focus on things that will promote growth realizing that ultimately God will grow you!

Lord, I thank You for giving my life joy and purpose. Please give me wisdom to see the work You're doing around me, and use me to promote Your work. Even though I am merely a fallible human being, help me to glorify You through my works. Amen.

義務的な思いで仕える機会を考えるのではなく、イエス様の姿にならうことができる素晴らしい機会としてとらえましょう。イエス様があなたにして下さったことを、もう一度思い起こしてみましょう。あなたが神様との歩みの中で喜びに満たされているなら、神様に仕えたい思いも自然にわいてくるでしょう。あなたの人生の目的の一つは、神様に仕え、神様の栄光を現すことです。ですから与えられている賜物を自分のためではなく、神様のためにという思いで一生懸命に用いる事が大切です。

まとめのことば

神様の最大のみこころは、人が救われ、霊的に成長することです。神様に仕え、クリスチャンとして成長し、キリストの満ち満ちた丈に達していきます。仕える中で、神様の栄光を現す事、自分を捧げる事、与えられたものを管理する事を体験し、また、望まれる周りの人との関係等について教えられる事がたくさんあるからです。そのような体験の中で、神様とはどういうお方なのか、そして神様に望まれる生き方について学んでいくのです。

第一コリント 3:6

「私が植えて、アポロが水を注ぎました。しかし、成長させたのは神です。」

覚えておくべき大切な視点は、「神様ご自身が成長させる」ということです。あなたがするべきことには一生懸命になり、結果は神様にゆだねて、成長させて頂きましょう。

　　　神様、私に生きる目的と喜びを与えて下さり感謝します。あなたが私の周りで起こそうとされている御業を悟る知恵を与えて下さい。そしてあなたの働きに私も加えて下さい。小さい者ですが、できる事を捧げる者として下さい。アーメン。

Step 14 The Importance of the Church

📖 Ephesians 1:22, 23

> *"And God placed all things under His feet and appointed Him to be head over everything for the church, which is His body, the fullness of Him who fills everything in every way."*

The word "Church" is derived from the Greek word "Ecclesia", meaning "a summoned congregation" or "brothers and sisters in the Lord," did not originally refer just to a building. The church is a gathering of people who were once dead in sin but have been saved by receiving Christ's salvation.

It's a spiritual community consisting of brothers and sisters in Christ. (John 1:12) You are a temple of the Holy Spirit, made purified and righteous. (I Corinthians 6:11, 19-20) The church is the body of Christ, and Christ is the head of the church. (Romans 12:5) The church is the fullness of Christ. (Ephesians 1:23) When you became a Christian, you became part of the church in the universal sense.

As people are called to Christ through the work of the Holy Spirit, they should become involved in a local, Bible believing church. It is in this place that people gather together to worship the Lord. It is a place where we can love God, seek His will, and love and serve one another.

📖 Ephesians 3:20, 21

> *"Now to Him who is able to immeasurably more than all we ask or imagine, according to His power that is at work within us, to Him be glory in the church and in Christ Jesus throughout all generations, forever and ever! Amen."*

Each church is ordained to reflect God's glory. Because your life was also created in order to show God's glory, you need to take seriously your connection to the church.

Step 14 教会の大切さ

📖 エペソ 1:22-23

> 「また、神は、いっさいのものをキリストの足の下に従わせ、いっさいのものの上に立つかしらであるキリストを、教会にお与えになりました。教会はキリストのからだであり、いっさいのものをいっさいのものによって満たす方の満ちておられるところです。」

「教会」とは、もともと建物自体を指すだけでなく「エクレシア」というギリシア語で「召し出された会衆」「主にある兄弟」という意味があります。それは、昔は罪の中に死んだ者であったが、今はキリストの救いを受け、特別に召されている者という意味であり、その人達の集まりが教会なのです。

教会とは、主にある兄弟姉妹との霊的なコミュニティー、共同体です（ヨハネ 1:12）。キリストの所有、聖霊の宮であって、清められ、義とされています（第一コリント 6:11，19，20）。教会はキリストの体であり、キリストは教会の頭です（ローマ 12:5）。教会は、キリストが満ち満ちているところです（エペソ 1:23）。救われた者達はすでに、普遍的な意味ではすでにキリストの体である「教会」の一員なのです。

又、一人ひとりがイエス様からの招きによって、それぞれの地域で集まっている地域教会にも大切な意味があります。御霊の働きによって救いを受けた者達が集い、主なるキリストを礼拝します。神様を愛し、神様ご自身のみこころを行う事を求め、互いを愛し合う場所です。

📖 エペソ 3:20-21

> 「どうか、私たちのうちに働く力によって、私たちの願うところ、思うところのすべてを越えて豊かに施す事のできる方に、教会により、またキリスト・イエスにより、栄光が、世々にわたって、とこしえまでありますように。アーメン。」

それぞれの教会は、神様の栄光が証しされるために与えられました。あなたの人生は神様の栄光を現すために創造されたのですから、教会を通して神様の栄光が現されるならば、あなたと教会の関わりも大切に考える必要があります。

God's glory is expressed by the church...

1: through worship in truth.

📖 **Psalm 48:1**

> *"Great is the Lord, and most worthy of praise, in the city of our God, his holy mountain."*

God is the Lord of all creation. Lovingly, He guides us to accomplish His great purpose through us. God desires praise and worship from people across the earth, and when someone worships in the Spirit and in truth (John 4:24), God is glorified.

Worship is an attitude of praising God. In a church worship service there may be times for praising God, praying, listening to the message, giving an offering, and taking communion. Each act is a part of worship and our actions praise the Lord. You should place a priority on worship and on offering it up to God. You don't go to a church to get spiritual energy, become cleansed from sin, or receive something.

An important thing to remember is that God is pleased by your worship "in spirit and truth", not by doing the ritualistic actions in worship. The Christians in the first church repented of their sins, accepted Christ, were baptized, and became disciples. They became devoted to Christ's teaching, fellowship, prayer, and to breaking of bread together. They had everything in common and continued to meet together with sincere hearts. The Lord added to their number daily with those who were being saved. (Acts 2:41-48) There was a sincere worship, Godly love for each other, and fellowship in unity. "Worship" means "to ascribe worth to". As you worship at your church, have a mindset of reverence, honor and awe for the Lord.

2: through spiritual growth.

The spiritual growth of the whole church is closely connected to the growth of each individual Christian who gathers there.

📖 **Ephesians 4:13**

> *"Until we all reach unity in the faith and in the knowledge of the Son of God and become mature, attaining to the whole measure of the fullness of Christ."*

神様の栄光が教会によって証しされるには、、、

1: 真の礼拝を通して

📖 **詩篇 48:1**
「主は大いなる方。大いにほめたたえられるべき方。」

神様は、全地の創造主であり、私たち一人ひとりを大きな目的と愛の中で導いて下さっています。神様とは、全地に、また人々にほめたたえられ、礼拝されるべきお方なのです。そのお方が霊とまことによって礼拝される時（ヨハネ 4:24）、神様の栄光、その素晴らしさは現わされるのです。

「礼拝」とは神様をほめたたえる姿勢を指します。教会での礼拝プログラム（儀式）には、賛美の時間、祈りの時間、メッセージを聞く時間、献金や聖餐式などが一般的に含まれるでしょう。それら一つ一つの時間は、神様をあがめる行為－礼拝－なのです。礼拝出席をあなたの生活の中で優先させ、神様のために特別にささげる時間としましょう。霊的な充電をするためや、清められるため、何かをもらうためなどに教会へ行くのではありません。

覚えておくべき大切な事は、礼拝儀式を行う事自体が重要なのではなく、「霊とまことによる礼拝」が最も神様に望まれているという事です。この地での最初の教会は、悔い改め、イエス様の救いを受け入れ、バプテスマを受け、キリストの弟子となり、教えを堅く守り、交わり、パンを裂き、祈っていました。いっさいの物を共有し、心を一つにして宮に集まり、賛美し、主も毎日救われる人々を仲間に加えてくださったのです(使徒の働き 2:41-48)。そこには、真の信仰にもとづいた心からの礼拝があり、兄弟姉妹を神様の愛で愛し、一致した交わりがあったのです。「礼拝」-Worship- とは、「価値あるものとみなす」という意味があります。あなたが大切に思い、あがめられるべきお方である唯一の神様を、最も価値あるものと認め、心からの礼拝を捧げるという思いを持ちつつ教会での礼拝にも出席しましょう。

2: 教会が霊的な成長をする事によって

教会全体の霊的成長は、そこに集う一人ひとりの神様の子達の成長と深く関わりがあります。

📖 **エペソ 4:13**
「ついに、私たちがみな、信仰の一致と神の御子に関する知識の一致とに達し、完全におとなになって、キリストの満ち満ちた身たけにまで成長するためです。」

First, all Christians need to grow in their faith, which is based on sound doctrine. It's imperative that everyone learns about sharing the Gospel and experiencing God's work of salvation through the church community. Additionally, through serving you can learn how to use your spiritual gifts for the Lord and train to become a true servant. (see Step 13: Serving God) Spiritual growth goes beyond mere church attendance or membership; it's about becoming a part of the body of Christ and making the expression of His glory your focus.

Of course, the degree of spiritual growth varies from person to person, but when you make church and unity in Christ the priority, the church grows and God's magnificence is displayed. The key to growing in faith is for the whole church to become one body and walk according to God's will. If each person and the community seeks to follow God's will, and puts it into practice, the community of God's children, the church, will be blessed.

3: through abiding in God's love and having unity in the Lord.

God's foundational command is to "love one another." Unity in the Lord brings love, support, encouragement, and consideration of one another. The church is a single body, which is built up through love. By loving one another and abiding in God's love together, the church consequently serves as a place where other people can also praise God. Also, when witnessing, a church can be available to the work of the Holy Spirit as you abide in the true love of God together. The unity of brothers and sisters in the Lord can be a powerful testimony to our faith. (Check John 13:34-35 and Step 12 The Art of Witnessing.)

Ephesians 4:16

"From Him the whole body joined and held together by every supporting ligament, grows and builds itself up in love, as each part does its work."

If everyone were to avoid the pursuit of his own interests and were sensitive to the needs of the other person instead, relationship would be filled with love. Because we are human, our relationships with others are continuously mingled with and influenced by our emotions. But when all the parts work together according to Christ, our relationships are built up and grounded in love. When God's love is present in relationships with others, God is glorified.

まず、正しい教理にもとづいた信仰の歩み方を身につけ、すべてのクリスチャンが聖書的に訓練されていく必要があります。そして、福音を伝え、神様の救いの御業を、教会という共同体を通して共に体験していくのです。また、奉仕を通して、喜びから神様にお仕えし、与えられた賜物を主のために用いる事を学び、真のしもべとして整えられていきます（賜物を用いることについては、Step 13「神に仕える」を参照）。そういった意味でも、ただ教会出席者でいるよりも、教会員となり、よりキリストの体の一部として、神様に栄光を帰す生き方、そして教会生活を念頭におく必要があるでしょう。

もちろん、個人個人によって信仰の成長度が違います。教会がこのような目的のもとキリストにある一致を目指す時、教会として成長している過程の中で、神様の素晴らしさがが現わされるでしょう。教会全体が一体となり神様のみこころに沿った歩みをするためにも、一人ひとりの信仰の成長は鍵となります。個々、そして群れとしての教会がみこころに従って歩むすることを望み、実践していくなら、きっとそのような神様の子達のコミュニティー、教会を祝福して下さるでしょう。

3: 神様の愛が交わりの中でとどまり、主にある一致が示される事によって

「互いに愛し合いなさい」とは、神様からの基本となる命令です。「互いに愛し合い」「励まし合い」「助け合い」「配慮し合っている体」とは主にある一致があるからこそ成されるものです。教会は、愛し合うことによって建て上げられていく共同体です。神様の愛を実践し、お互いの中に留まった神様の愛ゆえに、他の人達がまた神様をあがめる事のできる場でもあります。伝道する時も聖霊が働かれやすいように、群れとして真の神様の愛に留まるなら、主にある一致を大切にする兄弟姉妹は「共に」力強い証人として用いられるでしょう。（ヨハネ 13:34-35、第一ペテロ 3:8、第一ヨハネ 4:20-21、Step 12「証人となる素晴らしさ」を参照。）

📖 エペソ 4:16

> 「キリストによって、からだ全体は、一つ一つの部分がその力量にふさわしく働く力により、また、備えられたあらゆる結び目によって、しっかりと組み合わされ、結び合わされ、成長して、愛のうちに建てられるのです。」

それぞれが、自分の利益を求めず、相手の必要に敏感になり「与える」態度を大切にするなら、その交わりはどんなに愛に満ちたものになるでしょう。人間ですから、色々な感情をまじえながら、人と関わって行きます。しかし「キリストによって」それぞれの部分が働く時、尊い結び目により、愛にもとづいた交わりが建て上げられるのです。それは、神様による御業ですから、その神様の愛が人間関係の中で示される時に、神様の栄光が現されるのです。

Hebrew 10:25

"Let us not give up meeting together, as some are in the habit of doing, but let us encourage one another – and all the more as you see the Day approaching."

Without fellowship with other Christians, you can't put God's love into practice. Work on ways to strengthen your relationships with other Christians. You might feel like separating from the church when you stumble by focusing on man rather than God. However, you should pray that through the foundation of the Gospel you can express God's love toward your brothers and sisters in Christ.

To learn more about God's family, look at Step 11 Relationships with Christians.

Summary

Church is a spiritual community to display God's glory, and it is necessary for your spiritual life. Worshipping Him in truth, praising and serving God, giving thanks, maintaining fellowship with other Christians, and witnessing together are all reasons to be a part of a church, the body of Christ. With the objective of being continuously filled by Christ and continuing to grow, the church will help you to love God, serve Him, and live a Spirit-filled life.

Lord Jesus, head of the church, please show me what I can do in order to show Your glory through the church. I pray that You would help me to make praising You my priority, and please show me how I can serve You. In my relationships with other Christians, help me to be a person who continuously expresses Your love. May others see Christ in me. Amen.

ヘブル 10:25

「ある人々のように、いっしょに集まる事をやめたりしないで、かえって励まし合い、かの日が近づいているのを見て、ますますそうしようではありませんか。」

神様の愛を実践するために、クリスチャンとの交わりを大切にしましょう。ここでのポイントは、交わる、ということ。困難さについては、ポイントがずれる。

交わりについて詳しくは、Step11「クリスチャンとの交わり」を参照。

まとめのことば

教会は神様の栄光が帰されるき所であり、あなたの信仰生活に欠かせないコミュニティーです。神様を真に礼拝し、感謝を捧げ、霊的な時を持ち、仕え、また、他のクリスチャンと交わりを保ち、共に伝道していくためにも、キリストの体である教会の一部となっていきましょう。あなた自身がキリストの満ち満ちた身たけにまで成長していく事を目標とし、教会を通して、神様をますます愛し、仕え、聖霊に満ちた生活を送りましょう。

教会のかしらであるイエス様、あなたの栄光が教会を通してますます現されるために、私ができる事を示して下さい。心から礼拝する思いを与えて下さい。礼拝へ出席する事を優先できるように助けて下さい。あなたに仕えるためにするべき事を示して下さい。またクリスチャンとの交わりの中で、あなたの愛を示して行く者とならせて下さい。アーメン。

Step 15 Becoming like Christ

📖 Colossians 3:10

"Put on the new self, which is being renewed in knowledge in the image of its Creator."

📖 Ephesians 4:15

"Instead, speaking the truth in love, we will in all things grow up into Him who is the Head, that is, Christ."

Only human beings were created to resemble God (Genesis 1:26). Unlike animals and nature, a human has a soul, intellect, and conscience as well as the capacity to think, feel emotions, make judgments, and solve problems. For these reasons we must use these characteristics responsibly.

One of God's ultimate purpose for your life is, in a spiritual sense, to become a person resembling Christ who has an eternal nature. You are a person who was reconciled by the cross and redeemed by Christ's salvation. Because you have eternal life, you won't perish. Also, in this life on earth, He desires for you to mature spiritually, becoming more Christ-like. Through the Step Lessons we have learned about reading the Bible, praying, battling against sin, seeking God's will, facing trials, witnessing, and serving. They are all important parts of spiritual growth helping you to know God. They enable us to live according to His will and become more Christ-like.

If you understand the purpose of the life you have been given, then you should focus on fulfilling that purpose. Let's learn about these things in order to live a life glorifying to God.

1: What it means to become like Christ

First, let's look at "Becoming Christ-like" with an earthly perspective. It means that you are growing in character and bearing the fruit of the Spirit (John 15). It is to seek after what God originally intended humans to be. By transformation and growth in your character, you become more like Christ. Also, you are to respond to the great commission to make disciples of Christ. (Matthew 28:19-20) Jesus lived as a human in order to serve as the ideal example for us. God's desire is not for us necessary to have a comfortable life, but a life that is becoming more like Christ daily.

Step 15 キリストの似姿に変えられる

📖 コロサイ 3:10

「新しい人を着たのです。新しい人は、造り主のかたちに似せられてますます新しくされ、真の知識に至るのです。」

📖 エペソ 4:15

「。。。あらゆる点において成長し、かしらなるキリストに達することができるためなのです。」

人間だけが神様に似せて造られました（創世記 1:26）。自然や動物と違って、人間には霊的、知的、道徳的な能力などが与えられているので、様々な事を考え、感じ、判断し、問題解決したりできます。だからこそ、それらの能力を正しく使う事に責任を負っているのです。

神様があなたに対して持っておられる目的の一つは、霊的な意味では、永遠というご性質を持ったイエス様の似姿に変えられる事です。それは、十字架によって和解され、贖われた、永遠に朽ちる事のない姿です。またこの世の人生においては、あなたが霊的、人格的に成長し、イエス様に似た者となっていく事です。聖書を読む事、祈る事、罪と戦う事、みこころを求める事、試練を経験する事、証しする事、仕える事などこれまでのStepで学んだすべては、あなたが神様を知り、神様のみこころの中で生きながら、イエス様のように変えられる生き方を求めて行くために大切な事項なのです。

与えられた人生の目的がわかれば、その目的を全うするために立てるべき人生のゴール、「目標」が決まります。神様のみこころにかなった人生を送るために、このことについて学んでみましょう。

1: キリストの似姿に変えられるとは

まず初めに、この世における観点において、「キリストの似姿に変えられる」事について見ていきましょう。これは、イエス様にとどまる事によって（ヨハネ 15 章）、あなたの品性が変えられ、人格的に成長することです。神様が人間に本来意図された姿を追求することとも言えます。またイエス様が仕えたように人々に仕え、弟子をつくりなさいとの呼びかけに（マタイ 28:19－20）答えていくことも含まれます。イエス様は、人が生きるための模範をたくさん見せて下さいました。神様があなたに望んでおられるのは、快適に送れる生活ではなく、日々イエス様にとどまり、イエス様のように変えられていくことです。

When you hear "become like Christ," you might get the impression that this means the dissolution of your personality and way of life, but this is not about losing the way you are. Rather, discover who you really are as a new creature in Christ. Grow in Him and discover God's purpose for you. As you experience things that help you become more like Christ, you will discover how you were created to be and will rejoice in praising God.

When you put into practice the things that you have been learning, you will certainly become more like Christ. Some examples of the transformation of your character would be:

- bearing fruit of the spirit (Fruit of your character – love, joy, peace, patience, kindness, goodness, honesty, gentleness, self-control) (Galatians 5:22)
- showing humility, gentleness, seeking justice, being compassionate, having a clean heart, promoting peace, and others (Matthew 5:1-12)
- reflecting faith, virtue, knowledge, self-control, perseverance, piety, brotherly love, and other attributes of God's love we have been given (II Peter 1:5-8)
- practicing God's unconditional love (I John 4:18,19, I Corinthians 13:4-8)
- To do good works in God's will. (Ephesians 2:10)

In addition to others, when we look at Christ's way of life there are always many more things to learn.

When we forget the ultimate goal of eternity, we become dissatisfied and complain about our circumstances, lose our endurance, and have a negative attitude. But because as children of God we are given clear objectives, we should persevere through these struggles while having faith in God.

There are many difficulties and trials in everyone's lives. However, there's not one that God doesn't know about. And through each thing you experience, God has a plan to change you into a person more like Christ. When you step forward in faith, the Holy Spirit will move in you. God can easily accomplish whatever He desires, so work at turning your heart toward God. Because you have strength in Christ, do the things God has perfectly expressed in His Word without worrying about how you feel. Move forward while only boasting of your weakness.

Second, 'Becoming Christ-like' requires an eternal perspective. That's because life on this earth is not the end for God's children. God has an eternal plan for you. Your life here, including death, is but a point along the road to God's heavenly, eternal kingdom (Philippians 3:20).

「キリストのようになる」と聞くと、自分の生活や個性がなくなってしまう印象を受けるかもしれませんが、「あなたらしさ」を失うわけではありません。むしろ、神様に意図されて創造された本当のあなたらしさを発見し、神様に喜ばれるより精錬させられたあなたをを見つけるでしょう。そして、イエス様のように変えられることを経験する時、あなたは造られた者として人生の意味を見い出し、神様をほめたたえる喜びで満ちるでしょう。

今までのStepで学んで来た事項を実践して行く時、あなたの人生は確実にキリストの似姿へと変えられていくでしょう。もたらされる具体的な変化とは、例えば、

- 御霊の実（人格の実― 愛、喜び、平安、寛容、親切、善意、誠実、柔和、自制）が実る。（ガラテヤ 5:22）
- 謙遜、柔和、正しさを求める、あわれみ深い、心が清い、平和をつくる。（マタイ 5:1-12）
- 信仰、徳、知識、自制、忍耐、敬虔、兄弟愛、愛などの神様の性質にあずかる。（第二ペテロ 1:5-8）
- 仕える者として来られたキリストに倣って、神様がもつ無条件の愛を実践できる（第一ヨハネ 4:18-19、第一コリント 13:4-8）
- 神様のみこころにかなう、良い行いができるように整えられる。（エペソ 2:10）

などがあげられます。

他にも、イエス様の生き方を見る時、学ぶ事はまだまだたくさんあるでしょう。

イエス様に似た者へ変えられていくプロセスの中で、永遠の最終目的を忘れてしまう時、誰でも状況に振り回され不満を言い、忍耐力をなくし、物事に否定的になったりもします。しかし、神様の子どもであるあなたは、キリストの似姿に変えられていくという、はっきりとしたゴールが与えられています。ゴールに向かって神様を信頼しつつ日々歩み続けましょう。この世の人生において、たくさんの困難、試練がやって来ます。しかし神様に知られていないことは何一つありません。一つひとつの出来事を通して、神様は、あなたをイエス様の似姿へと変えて下さるご計画を持っておられます。信仰を持って踏み出す時に、聖霊があなたの内で働いて下さいます。聖霊なる神様が働かれやすいように、あなたも心を神様に向ける努力が必要です。感情が伴わなくても、正しいと示されている事を行い、（キリストによって強さとなる）自分の弱さを誇りながら前進しましょう。

次に、永遠の観点をもって、「キリストのように変えられる」ということを覚えておく必要があります。なぜなら、神の子にとっては、この世での人生がすべてではなく、神様の永遠のご計画の中にいるからです。死を含め、今歩んでいる人生は御国への通過点なのです。（ピリピ 3:20）

📖 II Corinthians 3:18

> *"And we all, who with unveiled faces contemplate the Lord's glory, are being transformed into his image with ever-increasing glory, which comes from the Lord, who is the Spirit."*

Other scriptures – I Corinthians 15:51-52, Ephesians 4:13-15, and James 1:4

Your life on this earth is not perfect. You will experience sadness, pain, and sufferings, but the Lord is with you as you go through trials. Remember that God's children have the hope of eternity. Keep striving to become more Christ-like, and trust His promise that you will be completely redeemed someday.

2: The truth about changing to resemble Christ

a) Desire to grow as a Christian takes effort.

Becoming saved did not require effort. However, growing as a child of God does require intentionally working toward this goal. The Bible says many things about the practice of striving toward this goal. (II Timothy 2:15, II Peter 1:5-8, Luke 13:24, and others) Change your sinful thoughts and actions, and learn the life that God desires for you. (Philippians 2:12) Depending upon the Holy Spirit, let's seek what God wants you to do.

b) God uses His Word, people, and circumstances in transforming us to become like Christ.

Step up until now, you've learned that God's word teaches you the truth, that your relationships with others are opportunities to practice God's love, and that challenging circumstances allow you to experience God's work. You learned that God intends for these situations to be opportunities for you to become more like Christ.

c) Testing and hardship are times of great growth.

When people experience difficulties, they ask God for help. There are certainly times where there's no choice but to leave the matter to God. In these kinds of circumstances, avoid a negative attitude and pray "What is God trying to teach me?" or "Please grow and change me." You will then be able to deal with these situations Christ's way. As you looked at II Peter 1:5-8, faith, self-control, and perseverance are things we often learn in times of trial. Let's consider it a joy, trusting in God's big plans.

> 📖 **第二コリント 3:18**
>
> *「私たちはみな、顔のおおいを取りのけられて、鏡のように主の栄光を反映させながら、栄光から栄光へと、主と同じかたちに姿を変えられて行きます。これはまさに、御霊なる主の働きによるのです。」*
>
> *その他、第一コリント 15:51−52、エペソ 4:13−15、ヤコブ 1:4 を参照。*

今、悲しみの中にいても、痛みの中にいても、困難の中にいても、この人生は不完全な状態です。もちろん、試練を通して慰め主である神様を体験していくのですが、神の子たちには永遠という希望があるのです。「永遠」という観点において、いつかはあなたも完全に贖われた姿となるという約束を覚えて、キリストのように変えられることを追求していきましょう。

2: キリストに似た者へ変えられる事の真理

a) 成長したいという願いと努力は必要。

救われるために努力は必要ありません。しかし、神様の子どもとして成長して行くためには、あなた自身が意図的に努力するべき事がたくさんあります。「励みなさい」「努力しなさい」「追い求めなさい」といった実践に向けての言葉が聖書にはたくさんみられます。（第二テモテ 2:15、第二ペテロ 1:5-8、ルカ 13:24 等）罪深い思いや行いを改め、神様が望まれる生き方を学び、実行していきましょう。（ピリピ 2:12）聖霊の働きにまかせて、神様があなたに求められていることに忠実でありましょう。

b) あなたがキリストのように変えられるために、神様は御言葉と人と状況を用いられる。

これまでの Step でも見て来たように、御言葉はあなたに真理を教え、周りの人との関係は神様の愛を実践する対象であり、様々な状況は神様の働きを経験させてもらえる機会です。一つひとつの機会がキリストの似姿に変えられていく成長の時として用いられる事を覚えて、神様に整えられていきましょう。

c) 試練と苦しみこそ、大きな成長の時。

困難にぶつかった時こそ、人は本当に神様を求めるようになります。あなたにも、神様に道をゆだねざるをおえない状況が必ず起こるでしょう。そういった状況の中で否定的になるのではなく、「今この事を通して、神様は私に何を学ばせようとしておられるのか」、また「私（の心）を造りかえて下さい」と祈れるようになれば、神様に望まれたあり方で問題に対処できるでしょう。先ほど見ました第二ペテロ 1:5−8 に見られる、信仰、自制、忍耐、なども試練の時によく学ばされるものです。神様の大きなご計画を信頼し、試練を喜びと思えるようになりましょう。

d) Growing takes time.

Becoming like Christ is a lifelong process. It's important to follow God's will as He reveals to you. Jesus said, " I am the vine, and you are the branches." Make it your priority to remain in Christ, for then, God will provide fruit in your life.

Summary

God is not concerned about what job you have, where you live, or what you own, but rather what kind of a child of His you are. Becoming more like Christ is accomplished through the process of experiencing God and following His will. Everything you have learned up until now has this final objective. No matter the circumstances of your life, if you have a tight grasp on your purpose and base your life on Christ's values, you will be able to judge all things wisely. Make it your priority to live the life you have been abundantly given by the Lord according to His objectives. Let's press on toward the prize that Christ has prepared for us (Philippians 3:12-14)!

I John 2:28

"And now, dear children, continue in Him, so that when He appears we may be confident and unashamed before Him at His coming."

Lord, thank You for creating me and for helping me to grow through each thing You do in my life. Please make my character more like Yours through prayer and Your word. From here on I'm entrusting my life to You. Please make me into a person who rejoices in You. Amen.

d) 成長には時間がかかる。

キリストのように変えられていくことは一生のプロセスです。神様のみこころを知り、実践して行く事は大切ですが、急ぐ必要はありません。「わたしはぶどうの木で、あながたがは枝です。」とイエス様が言われたように、まず、御言葉に聞き、イエス様にとどまることを優先しつつ、実を結ばせて下さる神様の働きに期待しつつ歩んで行きましょう。

まとめのことば

神様は、あなたがどんな職業につくか、どこに住むか、何を所有するか等に一番関心があるのではなく、あなたが「どのような神様の子であるか」という事に最大の関心を持たれています。

キリストのように変えられていく事は、神様を体験し、神様のみこころを体験していくプロセスです。今まで学んで来たことすべては、この最終目標であるキリストに似る者へ変えられていく真理に至ります。あなたの状況がどのようであっても、人生の目標を、また、永遠の行き先をしっかりと握り締めているならば、イエス様の価値観を土台として、すべてのことを判断していけるでしょう。この与えられている人生を、より豊かに主のために生きれるように、目的に沿って優先順位をはっきりさせましょう。イエス様が準備して下さっている栄冠を得るために、目標をめざして走り続けましょう！（ピリピ3:12－14）

第一ヨハネ 2:28

「そこで、子どもたちよ。キリストのうちにとどまっていなさい。それは、キリストが現れるとき、私たちが信頼を持ち、その来臨のときに、御前で恥じ入るということのないためです。」

私の人生の造り主である神様、生活の中で起こる一つひとつの出来事を通して、私を成長させて下さい。御言葉を学び、祈りを通してあなたと交わり、ますますイエス様に似た者へと私の人格を造り変えて下さい。これからの人生もあなたにゆだねます。あなたに喜ばれる歩みを選択していける者として下さい。アーメン。

Made in the USA
Middletown, DE
28 December 2022